# Science Experiments

HINKLER BOOKS

Illustrator: Glen Singleton
Cover illustrator: Rob Kiely
Project editor: Katie Hewat
Designer: Diana Vlad

Published in 2009 by Hinkler Books Pty Ltd
45–55 Fairchild Street
Heatherton VIC 3202 Australia
www.hinklerbooks.com

ISBN: 978 1 7418 2119 2
Printed and bound in China

# Contents

3

# Introduction

This book is full of simple science experiments to shock and amaze you. Ordinary materials like vinegar, string, eggs and paper are used to make extraordinary things. They will help you find how science works, and why things happen the way they do. Most of all, these experiments are fun!

You will end up growing your own stalactites and be able to bounce an egg. Your kitchen will never be the same when you create your own underwater volcano.

Like to eat? Why not try baked ice cream? Yes, I do mean baked.

You will find most of the equipment you need for the experiments around the house. A good tip is to find an empty box and keep it stocked with things you might need. Don't throw out used jars, corks or lengths of string. Why not store them in the box all ready for when you do your next experiment?

# Acknowledgements

The experiments were tried, tested and improved by the following very giggly children during their holidays and weekends – they had loads of fun. We hope you do too! • Rebecca Chapman • Olivia Kenyon • Shivani Goldie • Katherine Jenkins • Verity Maton

A special thanks to the following big people too! • Dr Greg Chapman • Dr Kate Kenyon • Lois Goldthwaite • Dr Paul Maton • Ann Jenkins

Helen Chapman

## Experiment Rating

| Easy: | Medium: | Difficult: | Adult needed: |
|---|---|---|---|
|  |  |  | +  |

# The Bouncin' Egg

**Can an egg bounce without breaking?**
**Wait! Don't try it yet. Read what to do first.**

Rat's Rating

**You will need:**
eggs, water, vinegar, flashlight, bowl

## Rat's Helpful Hint

Don't do this experiment in a hot bath. The eggs will cook and get hard-boiled. Also, don't try this at the end of the week – eggs hate Fry-days.

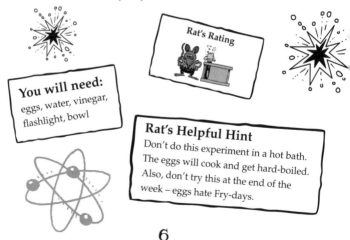

# What to do for this biology experiment

1   Put one whole raw egg in a glass of water.

2   Put one whole raw egg in a glass of vinegar.

3   The eggs are the same aren't they? Now, leave them for a few hours.

4   Look at both eggs. Do they still look the same? The egg in the water is the same, but the egg in the vinegar has changed. The shell has begun to fizz. The acid in the vinegar dissolves the calcium carbonate that's in the shell.

5   Look carefully. Does the egg in the vinegar still have its shell? Touch it. It now feels and looks like a rubber ball, doesn't it?

Hey! Go easy!

7

6 Leave both eggs alone for seven days. After that time, take the egg in vinegar to a dark room and shine a flashlight at it. What do you see? The light bounces off the egg, doesn't it?

8 Let the egg drop. Do you think it will splatter? Try it!

7 Take the egg out of the glass of vinegar. Hold the egg a little bit over a bowl.

## What Happens

Your egg bounces! Try it again getting a little higher each time. See how high you can make the egg bounce. What do you think will happen if you try to bounce the egg that was in the water? Hold it over the bowl and try.

## Why

- A chemical change takes place in the egg when left in vinegar.
- The vinegar, which is an acid, reacts with the calcium carbonate of the eggshell.
- The change makes the shell go soft, then disappear. This is called 'decalcification'.
- The egg in the glass of water does not chemically change.

Just look at those legs! She's been soaking them in VINEGAR... You can tell!

## Fun Fact

You can make chicken bones so soft that you can bend them. Put a clean wishbone or leg bone into a jar of vinegar. Make sure the bones are completely covered. Leave them there for seven days. The bones will go so soft that you can twist them into a knot! Minerals in the bone make it strong and rigid. The vinegar takes away these minerals and the bones dissolve like the eggshell.

## Mini Answer

It is known that vinegar was used in Babylon in 5,000 B.C.

## Mini Quiz

The word vinegar comes from two French words – 'vin' which means wine and 'aigre' which means sour. Vinegar has been in use for a long time, but how long?

9

# Grow a Stalactite

Have you ever been in a cave and seen amazing columns? These are 'stalactites' and 'stalagmites'. It takes many hundreds of years for these to grow. You can make your own in just a few weeks!

How long have you two been doing this?

Oh.... Only a couple of thousand years... But we're having a great time!

Rat's Rating

## You will need:
glass jars, baking soda or Epsom salts (the salts take longer but give you more shapes), spoon, wool/cotton/string (any thread that will soak up water), paperclips, water, saucer

### Rat's Helpful Hint
If you get a chance to visit a dark cave, remember to hide around a corner. When someone passes by, leap out and shout 'Boo!'. Adults just love this!

# What to do for this chemistry experiment

1. Fill two clean jars with hot water.

2. Add as much baking soda to each jar as will dissolve.

3. Mix well so that the soda is dissolved completely.

4. Dip each end of the thread into the jars. The ends must be weighed down with paperclips, pencils, icy pole sticks or nails to keep them in the jars.

5 Place a saucer between the jars to catch the drips.

6 Let the thread hang between the jars and over the saucer.

7 Leave the jars for two to three weeks. Will anything grow?

## What Happens

A white stalactite grows down from the wool and a stalagmite grows up from the saucer.

## Why

- The baking soda mix is carried up through the thread. This is called *capillary action*.
- The mix then drips onto the saucer.
- Over the days, the dripping water evaporates. It leaves a little of the baking soda behind.
- These bits of baking soda make a tiny stalactite and stalagmite.
- After months, these join. They make a single column like the one you see in a cave.

## Fun Fact

One of the world's tallest stalagmites is in Slovakia. Cavers found the 32.6 m (106.9 ft) tall stalagmite in 1964.

## Mini Quiz

What is the difference between stalactites and stalagmites?

DANGEROUS!

WHAT'S THE VIEW LIKE FROM UP THERE?

## Mini Answer

Stalactites are the long rock columns that grow from the roof of a cave and hang down. Stalagmites look the same but they grow on the bottom of a cave and grow upward. When they meet, they make a column. They come from deposits of the mineral calcium carbonate in water that drips into the cave. To remember the difference between the two, think of this: stalactites hold tight ('tite') to the roof of the cave and stalagmites might ('mite') reach the roof.

13

# Potato Obstacle Race

Like all plants, potatoes turn energy from the sun into food energy to help them live. But what happens if you block out most of the light with obstacles? Are potatoes smart enough to get past your obstacles and reach the light?

Rat's Rating

**You will need:**
shoe box with lid, a sprouting potato (one with little white shoots growing out of it), scissors, potting mix, 'obstacles' (small boxes, thread spools, lolly tubes, baby food jars), sunny days

# What to do for this biology experiment

1. Cut a small coin-sized gap in the short side of the box

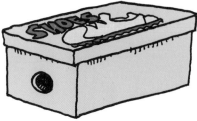

2. Put a handful of potting mix in the corner of the shoebox. It must be at the opposite end from the hole you made.

4. Put the 'obstacles' in the box. The smaller the box, the less obstacles you will need.

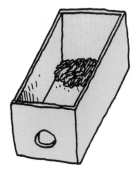

Hmmm
A nice and comfy piece of dirt

3. Lay the potato on the soil.

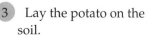

**5** Put the lid on. Place the box anywhere that gets lots of sun. Don't touch the box for four weeks.

**6** When the four weeks are up, open the box. What do you see?

## What Happens

The shoot has made its way over, or around the obstacles you left in the way and has reached the hole.

## Why

- Plants have cells that are sensitive to light. The cells show the plant which way to grow.
- A tiny bit of light came into the shoebox. The potato shoot twisted until it reached the light.
- Plants will always grow towards the light. Even if they are buried deep in the soil.
- The shoot should be green, but it's white. This is because the *chlorophyll* that makes it green can't be made in the dark shoebox.

16

## Mini Quiz

Why is it bad to eat potatoes that have turned green?

## Mini Answer

Green potatoes are poisonous if you eat too many. The green is a chemical called *solanine*. This is made when the potatoes are left in sunlight. Even fluorescent lights at supermarkets can make potatoes turn green. Potato 'eyes' also have lots of solanine, so don't eat them! When peeling potatoes, peel away all the green.

# Fuzz Balls

Can mould be useful in making medicine? Does bacteria have an infectious laugh? Let's find out.

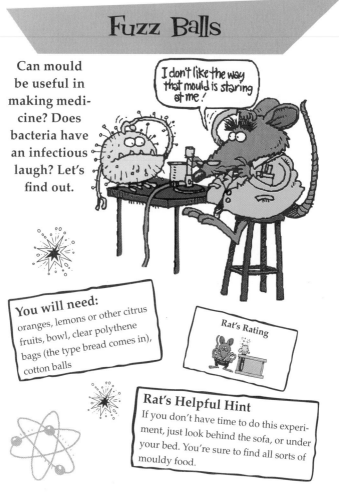

I don't like the way that mould is staring at me!

## You will need:
oranges, lemons or other citrus fruits, bowl, clear polythene bags (the type bread comes in), cotton balls

Rat's Rating

## Rat's Helpful Hint
If you don't have time to do this experiment, just look behind the sofa, or under your bed. You're sure to find all sorts of mouldy food.

# What to do for this botany experiment

1   Place the fruit in a bowl. Leave it out in the air for one day.

2   Open the two bread bags. Put one orange, one lemon and a wet cotton ball in each bag.

3   Tie the ends of the bags.

4   Place one bag in the refrigerator.

5   Place the other bag in a warm dark place.

6   Leave the bags closed for two weeks.

7   Check the fruit through the bags each day.

## What Happens

The fruit in the refrigerator looks much the same. At worst, it may be a bit drier. The other fruit has turned into blue-green fuzz balls. This fuzzy growth on the outside of the fruit is *penicillin*.

EEEEE... That's some mighty ugly citrus fruit!

## Why

- Mould is a form of fungus that makes tiny cells called *spores*.
- Spores are even tinier than dust particles! They float through the air.
- Mould grows faster in moist warm places. That is why foods become mouldier in the summer.
- Keeping food cool slows the growth of mould. Freezing keeps foods fresh for even longer periods.
- Fungi are all around us. They usually don't reach the fruiting body stage. This is because there aren't enough nutrients and water available.

Under a microscope, penicillin mould looks like a small brush. The Latin word for paintbrush is *penicillus*. This is how penicillin got its name. The word pencil also comes from this Latin word, because brushes were used for writing.

## Mini Quiz

How did an accident lead to the discovery that penicillin could kill bacteria?

You gotta see this! There's more than PENICILLIN living in your toothbrush! Where's it been?

In my MOUTH...

## Mini Answer

Alexander Fleming discovered penicillin by accident. In 1928, he left an open dish of bacteria in his laboratory and after two weeks found mould growing on the bacteria. He saw that there was a clear zone where the bacteria had died. Fleming discovered that the mould had made a chemical that could kill bacteria and cure infections. Penicillin is still used today as an *antibiotic* to fight some infections.

# Rock and Dissolve

**Can something as soft as rain dissolve something as strong as a rock?**

**You will need:**
half a glass of lemon juice, half a glass of vinegar, half a glass of water, 3 pieces of white chalk

Rat's Rating

## What to do for this chemistry experiment

**1** Take the glasses, which you have half filled with lemon juice, vinegar and water.

**2** Put one piece of chalk in each of the glasses. Make sure part of the chalk is in the liquid.

**3** Place the glasses where they won't be knocked over.

**4** Check on the glasses over the next few days. What is happening?

## What Happens

The chalk dissolves in the vinegar and in the lemon juice.

## Why

- When you breathe out, you expel carbon dioxide into the air.
- When carbon dioxide dissolves into raindrops, it makes rain become naturally acidic.
- Over time, this acid rain dissolves and erodes rocks.
- The chalk you used in the experiment is made of the rock limestone, or *calcium carbonate*.
- When acids react with limestone, they eat away at the rock and start to break it apart.
- Lemon juice and vinegar are acids. They're much stronger than acid rain, so erosion happens more quickly. You can see how acid rain can affect rocks over hundreds and thousands of years.

England's famous White Cliffs of Dover are made of great sheets of chalk, a form of calcium carbonate. If you lean against the cliffs, you get covered with white powder.

Stop rubbing yourself on the chalk cliffs and come play with your brother in the gravel... They'll use you at school to write on the blackboard!

## Mini Quiz

What does the Great Pyramid of Giza have to do with chalk?

## Mini Answer

The Great Pyramid is mainly made from blocks of limestone. The fine white limestone came from a quarry on the other side of the Nile. Egyptians used copper chisels to cut their way down into the limestone. They slowly separated block after block from the rock face.

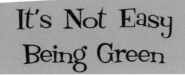

# It's Not Easy Being Green

*I think all you need is a little light my friend!*

'Leaf through' these green activities. You'll find that looking green doesn't always mean looking sickly.

Rat's Rating

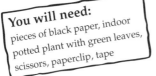

**You will need:**
pieces of black paper, indoor potted plant with green leaves, scissors, paperclip, tape

**Rat's Helpful Hint**
Make sure the plant you use is alive. If you use a fake one, not a lot will happen.

# What to do for this botany experiment

1. Cut two pieces of black paper big enough to cover one leaf on the plant.

2. Sandwich the leaf between the two pieces of paper.

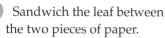

3. Clip the paper at the top and tape the sides.

4   Make sure that the leaf does not get any sunlight.

5   Wait for seven days.

6   Uncover the leaf. Does it look different compared to the rest of the plant?

## What Happens

The leaf is much paler than the other leaves on the plant. Now, watch the leaf over the next few days. See what happens to it when it gets sunlight again.

## Why

- If plants don't get sunlight, they can't make chlorophyll.
- Chlorophyll is the chemical that gives leaves their green colour.
- Without sunlight, the green pigment gets used up. It can't be replaced in the leaf. You end up with a leaf that loses its green colour, and will finally die.
- After a week without the covering, the leaf turns green again.

28

## Fun Fact

Leaves are nature's food factories. Plants take water from the ground through their roots. They take a gas called *carbon dioxide* from the air. Plants use sunlight to turn water and carbon dioxide into glucose. Plants use glucose for energy and growing.

I've just spent seven days in some kind of scientific experiment...so I'm out to get some sun...some water...and plenty of nice fresh carbon dioxide

## Mini Quiz

Do you find green plants living below 100 metres (328 feet) in the ocean?

## Mini Answer

No! Green plants only grow near the surface of the ocean. The deeper the water, the less plants are found. This is because green plants need sunlight. The sunlight totally disappears below 100 metres (328 feet) and the plants cannot live. Try something similar yourself. Put one plant in a sunny spot and another plant of the same variety in a dark cupboard and leave them for seven days. The plant in the cupboard will be lighter in colour and wilted.

# Super Starch

**Can something be a solid and a liquid at the same time? Sounds impossible! What do you think?**

Rat's Rating

**You will need:**
cornflour, measuring cup, mixing spoon, bowl

# What to do for this chemistry experiment

1. Place 1 cup of cornflour in a large bowl.

2. Add 1/4 – 1/2 cup of water and mix to a thick paste.

3. The powder is solid. The water is a liquid. Do you think the mixture will be a solid or a liquid?

4. Actually, it's both! With your hands, knead a handful of the mixture. It will become firm as long as you keep kneading.

5. Stop kneading. Quickly punch the mixture with your fist. It feels hard and may even crack.

31

6    Watch the mixture. Now that you have stopped
     kneading, it will return to its original form.

7    Push your fingers into it very slowly.
     They will slide in as though the
     mixture is a liquid. Raise your hands
     and see it pour through your fingers.

## What Happens

As it stands, the mixture is a liquid – it's just water
with powder floating in it. However, when you hit
it, the water molecules are forced into the middle of
each grain of powder, so the mixture is solid.

## Why

- Some fluid mixtures have two forms.
- *Isotropy* is when a liquid becomes solid when moved.
- You can see this when walking on wet sand. The
  sand firms up below your feet when you first walk.
  It then becomes more liquid as your feet sink into it
  a moment later. If you run over the sand, it will feel
  hard. If you walk slowly, your feet will sink below
  the surface with each step.
- *Thixotropy* is the opposite of *isotropy*. *Thixotropy* is when
  the liquid mixture becomes more liquid as it is moved.
- You might have done this when you hit the end of a
  tomato sauce bottle to get the tomato sauce to come
  out. The force temporarily makes the sauce 'runny'
  and it comes out easily from the bottle.

Do you know that when you drink water you're drinking dinosaur spit? The water we have today is the same water that the dinosaurs drank. How can this be? Well, it can take a water molecule thousands of years to finish a cycle from ocean to sky to land and back to the ocean again. This is because the water may be trapped in ice for a very long time.

## Mini Quiz

What does starch have to do with newspapers?

## Mini Answer

Starch is used as a binder in the making of paper. It's the use of a starch coating that controls how much ink comes through when printing. Cheaper papers don't use as much starch. This is why your fingers get black when you hold newspaper.

Does your water taste a little.... Prehistoric?

Sure does! A little Jurassic actually!

33

# Invisible Ink

"PAINTING IN INVISIBLE INK"
by I C. LITTLE

You've heard of secret messages written in code, haven't you? But have you heard of secret messages being written with invisible ink?

Rat's Rating

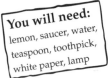

**You will need:**
lemon, saucer, water, teaspoon, toothpick, white paper, lamp

**Rat's Helpful Hint**
Why not send your invisible ink letter to a friend to read?

# What to do for this chemistry experiment

1 Squeeze the lemon juice into the saucer.

3 Dip the toothpick into the lemon juice mix. Not too much or you'll make invisible blobs!

2 Add a few drops of water and mix well with the spoon.

MIX MIX

4 Use the toothpick to write a message on ordinary white paper. Thick paper works best.

5 When it dries, the writing will be invisible.

6 Heat the paper by holding it with the written side down near a light bulb. If an adult is helping, you can use heat from a stove or candle. What do you see?

## What Happens

While it heats up, the invisible ink writing slowly becomes brown and visible. The words appear on the page.

*This message is no longer a SECRET!*

## Why

- The juice of lemons has compounds of *carbon*.
- These compounds have almost no colour when you dissolve them in water.
- When you heat them, the carbon compounds break down and turn black.

My old lemons were flat in my flashlight... So I'm installing fresh ones

## Mini Quiz

How does squeezing lemon juice onto fruit salad keep it fresh?

## Mini Answer

When cut fruit like apples, pears and bananas are left out in the air, they turn brown. This is because they react with the oxygen in the air. They become *oxidised*. Lemons contain vitamin C (ascorbic acid). Ascorbic acid slows the reaction between the chemicals in the fruit and the oxygen in the air. This keeps the colour and taste of the other fruit.

# Red Cabbage Rules

An *indicator* is a chemical that changes colour when an acid or alkali is added to it. Try making your own indicators and find out how to measure different substances.

Rat's Rating

## You will need:
small red cabbage, grater, bowls, water, saucepan, jug, strainer, paper towels/coffee filters, sheet of white paper, coloured pencils, solution liquids to test (lemon and orange juice, vinegar, milk, tap water, soapy water), glasses/paper cups

## Rat's Helpful Hint
To stop your indicator strips from growing mouldy, freeze them in bags. Remember to label the bag. If not, you may find yourself sucking on cabbage flavoured icy poles!

## What to do in this chemistry experiment

1. Grate half a small red cabbage. Let the gratings sit in a bowl of water for several hours. Drain the red cabbage water into another bowl. Or, to fast-track the process, put the grated cabbage into a saucepan with just enough water to cover it. Ask an adult to put the pan on the stove. Boil for 20–30 minutes, until the liquid turns a dark purple colour.

2. Let the cabbage juice cool and then strain it into a jug.

4. Soak the strips of paper in the red cabbage juice until they turn bluish purple.

3. Cut 5 cm (2 in) strips of paper towels.

5   Lay the wet strips flat on a bench and leave them to dry. These are your indicator strips.

6   Put the liquids into separate paper cups.

7   Dip your paper indicator strips into the liquids.

8   Using pencils and the white paper, copy down the colour that the paper strip turns.

9   Draw a picture, or write the name of the liquid that made the paper turn that colour.

10  Use your notes to make a chart to show the different colours that different liquids turn the paper strips.

MY INDICATOR CHART

| LEMON | ORANGE | VINEGAR | MILK |
|---|---|---|---|
| TAP WATER | SOAPY WATER | pH TESTER | |

## What Happens

Your cabbage juice is a simple pH tester. It reacts differently to different substances. Once you know what colour the juice turns in acids and alkalis, you can use it to test some other liquids.

## Why

- Red cabbage has pigments that react differently to acids and alkalis.
- When you dip your strips into your substance and wait a few minutes, the colour will fully develop.
- Your indicator strips will turn red-yellow in acid, green in neutral and purple-blue in alkali.

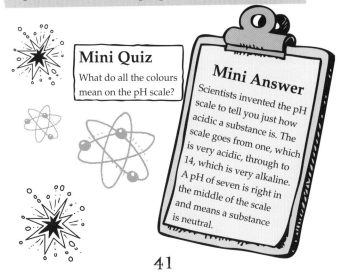

### Mini Quiz

What do all the colours mean on the pH scale?

### Mini Answer

Scientists invented the pH scale to tell you just how acidic a substance is. The scale goes from one, which is very acidic, through to 14, which is very alkaline. A pH of seven is right in the middle of the scale and means a substance is neutral.

# Blow Your Top

Have you seen a real volcano erupt? Well, make your own. It's much safer.

## You will need:
flour, salt, cooking oil, water, large bowl, clean plastic bottle, baking pan, food colouring (red looks good), liquid detergent, baking soda, vinegar, water

Rat's Rating

## Rat's Helpful Hint
This is a messy experiment. Make sure you know who's going to be cleaning up. Don't let your dog be the one to lick up the mess.

## What to do in this chemistry experiment

**1** Mix 6 cups of flour, 2 cups of salt, 4 tablespoons of cooking oil and 2 cups of water in a large bowl.

**3** Stand the bottle in the baking pan.

**4** Mould the salt dough around the bottle. Make sure you don't cover up the bottle mouth or drop any dough in the bottle. You can build your volcano with as much detail as you like, or leave it plain.

**2** Using your hands, mix the ingredients until smooth and firm. Add more water to the mixture if needed.

**5** Fill the bottle almost to the top with warm water.

**6** Add drops of food colouring until you get a colour you like.

**7** Squeeze 6 drops of the liquid detergent into the bottle.

**8** Add 2 tablespoons of baking soda.

**9** Slowly pour vinegar into the bottle and jump back quickly. What do you think will happen?

**What Happens**
The 'lava' flows out of your volcano.

VESUVIUS erupting NOW!

44

## Why

- Mixing baking soda and vinegar makes a chemical reaction.
- A chemical reaction is where one substance is chemically changed to another.
- All chemical reactions are about the making or destroying of bonds between atoms in which carbon dioxide gas is made – the same gas that bubbles in a real volcano.
- The gas bubbles build up in the bottle. They force the liquid 'lava' mixture up and over the mouth of your volcano.

## Fun Fact

Over the long term, volcanic eruptions can help us. Volcanic materials break down to form fertile soil rich in minerals.

## Mini Quiz

Where does the word 'volcano' come from?

Yep! This should be a great place for a farm... in about A MILLION YEARS

## Mini Answer

The word 'volcano' comes from the island of Vulcano, near Sicily in Italy. A century ago, the local people believed that Vulcano was the chimney of the forge of Vulcan. Vulcan was the blacksmith of the Roman gods.

# Wax Factor

Can you make a new candle from
bits and pieces of old ones?

## You will need:
pieces of old, used white candles, old, used wax crayons, pan, string, spoon, skewer, paper cup

Rat's Rating

# What to do in this chemistry experiment

1  Put the candles and the wax crayons in a pan.

2  Ask an adult to melt them slowly over a low heat. Stir gently to swirl the mix together.

3  While the wax is melting, make a small hole in the bottom of a paper cup with a skewer.

4  Thread the string through.

5  Tie a knot underneath. The string should be long enough so you can hang your candle to dry.

47

6 Ask an adult to pour the wax into the paper cup.

7 Hang it up by its long string to dry. What happens?

## What Happens

The wax will turn hard. To use your new candle, snip the string at the top and the bottom. Leave just enough at the top to use for the wick. It is very IMPORTANT to remove the paper cup before you light your new candle.

## Why

- Wax can change from a solid to a liquid when it is heated.
- It will become a solid again when it cools.

## Fun Fact

On Earth, gravity-driven buoyant convection makes a candle flame a teardrop-shape. This means that the air in the flame expands and becomes lighter. The lighter air rises. This is the convection current. In microgravity, there are no convective flows. The candle flame is round because the vapourised wax spreads out from the wick and the oxygen goes into the flame from surrounding air.

## Mini Quiz

Where do candles come from?

## Mini Answer

Candles came from the Romans. Ancient Egyptians used tallow-soaked torches, but the Romans had candles with a wick. These were used to help people travel through dark nights, and for lighting homes and places of worship.

# Gelatin Mobile

Gelatin is used to make pill capsules, heart valves, photographic film and, of course, fruit-flavoured desserts. But can you make a mobile with it?

> You're going to have to stop being so nervous and stop wobbling like jelly... you'll ruin the photo!

## You will need:

plain gelatin, water, food colouring, plastic lid with rim, saucepan, egg slice, paper towels, cookie cutters, drinking straw, scissors, cooling rack

Rat's Rating

## Rat's Helpful Hint

Why not colour your mobile to match a festivity such as orange for Halloween, red for Valentine's Day or green for St Patrick's Day?

# What to do in this chemistry experiment

1  Put 75 ml (5 table-spoons) of water and 3–5 drops of food colouring in the saucepan.

2  Ask an adult to put the saucepan over a low heat.

3  Tip in three envelopes of unflavoured gelatin and stir until it dissolves.

4  Cook and stir for 30 seconds or until the mixture is thick.

5  Pour the mixture into a plastic lid with a rim.

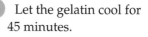

6  Push the air bubbles out with a spoon.

7  Let the gelatin cool for 45 minutes.

8  Use an egg slice to carefully lift the gelatin from the lid. What have you made?

51

## What Happens

You have made an elastic gel. Use the cookie cutters to make different shapes. Scissors are great for making spirals. Make holes in the gel with a plastic drinking straw so you can hang your shapes. Dry your shapes on a cooling rack, or hang them on string to dry. The gelatin will be hard like plastic in two to three days.

## Why

- Gelatin is actually a protein called *collagen*.
- Collagen molecules line up to make fibres. These fibres don't dissolve in water.
- The fibres form a network that hold cells in place.
- When collagen is heated it breaks down to make a simpler protein called gelatin.
- Gelatin does dissolve in water. When a gelatin solution cools, it makes a semi-solid mass or gel.
- A network of gelatin molecules trap the water in gelatin. It does this in much the same way as collagen molecules trap water.

## Fun Fact

When connected to an EEG (electroencephalogram), gelatin shows movement almost the same as the brain waves of a healthy adult.

EEG

I'm picking up excessive brain waves! ...What are you worrying about?

A bowl... a spoon ...ice cream and custard!

## Mini Quiz

Where does gelatin come from?

## Mini Answer

Gelatin is extracted by boiling in water (or acid) the bones, tissue, hooves and ligaments of slaughtered meat-producing animals.

# Twister

Can there ever be a place where inside and outside are one and the same?

**You will need:**
sheet of paper, scissors, pen, masking tape

Rat's Rating

## What to do in this topology experiment

1. Cut the paper into a long rectangle about 2 cm (1 in) wide.

2. Hold the strip out straight.

3. Give it a half twist (180 degrees). Use the masking tape to stick the two ends together.

4. Hold the edge of the strip against the tip of a pen.

5. Draw a line down the centre of the strip. Don't take the pen off the paper.

6. Turn the paper and keep on drawing the line. You will move the paper as you go along. Do not stop until your line meets up with your starting point.

55

(7) Take off the masking tape. Look at the paper. What have you done?

## What Happens

You have drawn on both sides of the paper without lifting your pen! Now, tape it back how it was before (with a half twist). With the scissors cut the strip along the centre line that you drew. Can you guess what you will make? You have made a chain that is twice as long as your original loop!

## Why

- Your shape is known as a *Möbius* strip.
- When you twisted your strip, the inside and outside became one continuous surface.
- When you cut the strip, it became one longer chain. But it still had only one continuous surface.
- Now, try the experiment again. This time give the paper a full twist. You'll be surprised at what you see.

## Fun Fact

During the early 1800s, the German mathematician August Möbius helped develop a study in geometry that is known as *topology*. Topology explores the properties of a geometrical figure that do not change when the figure is bent or stretched.

I don't know what I'm making! I was going to call it a MÖBIUS STRIP... But I think I'll just call it .... a mess!

## Mini Quiz

Can Möbius strips be used for anything?

## Mini Answer

Möbius strips have been used as fan belts in cars and conveyor belts in factories. You'll find them being used as continuous loop recording tapes. This doubles the playing time of the tapes.

# The Suspenseful Egg

Can you imagine something that doesn't float or sink when put in a liquid?

Rat's Rating

# What to do in this forces experiment

1  Half fill a glass jar with water. Put a raw egg into the jar. It sinks, doesn't it?

2  Take out the egg.

3  Add 2 teaspoons of salt to the water. Mix well.

**4** Take the same egg and put it in the jar. Watch the egg. What happens?

## What Happens

If there is enough salt in the water, the egg will float.

## Why

- The egg floats in salt water because of density (weight divided by the amount of space it occupies). The egg has greater density than fresh water, so it sinks.

Seventy-five percent of the earth's surface is water. Of all that water, 97 percent of it is salt water. We can't drink salt water. It is hard and costs a lot of money to remove salt from water to make it drinkable.

## Mini Quiz

Why does ocean water contain salt?

## Mini Answer

As water flows in rivers, it picks up small amounts of mineral salts from the rocks and soil of the riverbeds. This slightly salty water flows into the ocean. The water in the ocean only leaves by evaporating and freezing as polar ice, but the salt stays dissolved in the ocean. It does not evaporate. The water that's left grows saltier and saltier as time passes.

# Candles Rock

The centre of gravity is that point in an object where there is as much weight on one side as the other.

Rat's Rating

# What to do in this forces experiment

1. Scrape away some wax from the flat end of the candle so you can see the wick.

2. Push a long nail through the exact middle of the candle.

3. Rest the nail over both glasses.

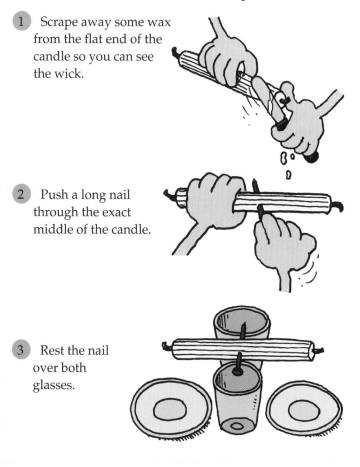

4. Put the saucers under each end of the candle.

5. Now you have a seesaw, but can you make it rock?

6. Ask an adult to light the wicks at both ends. Watch and see what happens.

## What Happens
The candle rocks up and down.

## Why
- A drop of hot wax falls from one end of the candle. This end rises because it is a bit lighter. Moments later, a drop falls from the other end of the candle and so it goes on.
- The balance of the candle is always being upset. This results in the candle continuing to rock up and down.

## Fun Fact

If you lay a potted plant on its side and leave it for a week, something amazing happens. The plant's stem will turn upwards! Plants have a chemical called auxin. This makes plant cells grow long. Gravity pulls the auxin down. This builds up along the bottom of the stem. The cells grow longer where the auxin build-up makes the stem turn upward.

OK! Obviously a plant with more than its fair share of AUXIN!

## Mini Quiz

Do men and women have a different centre of gravity?

## Mini Answer

Yes, they do! Most women have their centre of gravity in the hip area. Men have it in their upper body. Try it yourself. Stand with your toes touching a wall. Place one foot behind the other. Take three steps back from the wall. Have someone place a stool between you and the wall. Lean over and place the top of your head against the wall. Your legs should be at a 45-degree angle with your body.

Holding the edge of the stool, pick it up and hold the seat against your chest. Keeping the stool against your chest try to stand up. If you have a low centre of gravity (female), the weight of the stool will not stop you standing up. If you have a high centre of gravity (male), the weight of the stool makes you so top heavy that you can't stand up.

# Pen Cap Submarine

How can a submarine sink in the ocean, then rise again and float on top?

**You will need:**
small clear plastic bottle, modelling clay, plastic pen cap, water

Rat's Rating

## What to do in this forces experiment

1. Fill the clean plastic bottle with water.

2. Attach a piece of modelling clay to the arm of a plastic pen cap.

3. Put the cap in the bottle so that it floats.

4. Put the lid on the bottle. It must be tight so that air doesn't leak from the bottle.

5. Squeeze the sides of the bottle. What do you think will happen?

## What Happens

The pen cap sinks when you squeeze the sides of the bottle.

## Why

- When you squeeze the bottle, you make more pressure inside.
- This forces more water up into the pen cap.
- The added water in the pen cap makes it weigh more. This makes the cap sink.
- A submarine works in much the same way. Each submarine has tanks that can be filled with water or air.
- When filled with air, the submarine will float on the surface of the water.
- When the submarine dives, large amounts of water are pumped into the tanks. This makes it much heavier.
- By regulating the amount of water and air in the tanks, the crew of the submarine can make it rise or sink to whatever level they want.

In the bathtub, pierce a hole in the lid and bottom of a plastic bottle. Push a plastic tube through the hole in the lid. Put your finger over the hole in the bottom. Fill the bottle to the top with water. Screw on the lid. Let the bottle sink to the bottom of the bath. Take your finger away from the hole and blow into the tube. Your mini-sub will rise to the surface.

## Mini Quiz

Are submarines a modern invention?

## Mini Answer

No! Greeks and Romans wrote about diving bells, and so did medieval writers. An English inventor described a workable submarine in 1578 and a Dutch inventor finally built oar-driven submarines in the early 1600s.

# Kaboom

**How can water float on water? Make your own underwater volcano and find out.**

## You will need:
small glass bottle, water, food colouring, string, large glass jar (big enough for the bottle to fit inside), scissors

Rat's Rating

## What to do in this heat experiment

**1** Cut a long piece of string. Tie one end tightly around the neck of the bottle.

**3** Pour cold water into the large glass jar until it is about three-quarters full.

**4** Fill the small glass bottle with hot water.

**2** Tie the other end of the string around the neck of the bottle to make a loop.

**5** Add food colouring – red looks good!

6  Hold the bottle by the
   loop of the string.

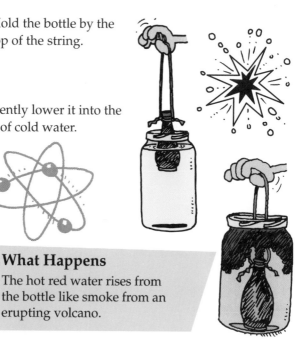

7  Gently lower it into the
   jar of cold water.

### What Happens
The hot red water rises from
the bottle like smoke from an
erupting volcano.

### Why
- The water looks as if it is still, but it isn't!
- Its molecules are always moving.
- Molecules move more quickly when they are
  hot.
- Hot water always rises to the surface and floats
  on the cold water.
- Cooler molecules sink.

The mid-oceanic ridge system is the longest mountain range in the world. The continuous mountain range is 65,000 km (40,400 mi) long and the total length of the system is 80,000 km (49,700 mi). Nearly every day, at least one underwater volcano erupts.

## Mini Quiz

How can a volcano erupt under water?

## Mini Answer

An underwater volcano can erupt under water because it is not a fire. Fire is a chemical reaction. It needs oxygen to keep going. If you put a fire under water, you take away the source of oxygen. The chemical reaction stops. Underwater volcanoes are very different. What you see on the surface is material that is already hot. It doesn't need any reaction at the surface to make it hot. There isn't any way for the water to 'put out' the eruption. This is because the water is changed to steam, which then explodes.

73

# The Drip

Which runs faster: hot or cold water? Hot runs faster because you can't catch a hot, but you can catch a cold!

**You will need:**
paper cups, pins, small drinking glass, water, ice cubes

Rat's Rating

# What to do in this temperature experiment

1. In the middle of the bottom of two paper cups, make a tiny pinhole. Make sure they are the same size.

2. Stand the paper cups on top of the glasses.

3. Pour very cold water into one glass until it's half full.

4. Add a few ice cubes to make sure it is really cold.

5  Pour hot water into the other glass until it is also half full. Watch as water drips from the paper cups into the glasses. Do you see any differences?

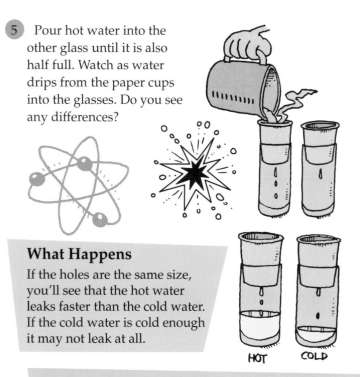

HOT    COLD

## What Happens

If the holes are the same size, you'll see that the hot water leaks faster than the cold water. If the cold water is cold enough it may not leak at all.

## Why

- Molecules exist although we can't see them.
- The molecules in hot water move faster than in cold water.
- The faster they move, the easier it is for them to slip past each other. That is why hot water is more likely to leak than cold.

76

## Fun Fact

You can see molecules with the help of food colouring. Get two drinking glasses that are exactly the same. Put half a cup of water in each of them. One glass should have cold tap water and the other hot tap water. Put two drops of food colouring in each glass. Time how long it takes for each of the colours to spread in the water. Molecules make the colours spread.

## Mini Answer

Molecules are so small that it is almost impossible to see them, even with a powerful microscope. But scientists know how to make models of molecules. The models help scientists study how molecules interact.

## Mini Quiz

What do molecules look like?

# Pop Goes the Popcorn

Why does popcorn pop? Grab an adult to help you find out. This experiment is hot!

O.K.! All I need now is a fizzy drink and a movie... to make this experiment complete!

## You will need:
unpopped popcorn, a medium pan with a clear lid, at least enough popcorn to cover the bottom of the pan one kernel deep, 1/3 cup of oil for every cup of kernels (don't use butter), stove

Rat's Rating

# What to do in this temperature experiment

1 Put the oil into the pan.

2 Place the pan on the stove.

3 Ask an adult to heat the oil so that it is very hot (if the oil smokes, it is too hot).

4 Test the oil on a couple of kernels. When they pop, add the rest of the corn.

5 Ask an adult to cover the pan and shake it so the oil spreads evenly.

6 Watch the shape and size of the corn kernels as they are heated.

7 When the popping begins to slow, ask an adult to take the pan away from the stovetop. The heated oil will still pop the rest of the kernels.

## What Happens

The corn kernels change from small, hard, orange kernels to big, soft, white shapes.

## Why

- The tough outside of the unpopped kernel is the *pericarp*. This is the part that often gets stuck between your teeth when you eat popcorn.
- The inside is full of starch. This grows into the white fluffy popcorn.
- The small amount of water inside the kernel makes this happen. As the kernel is heated, the water evaporates. It changes to a gas. The gas grows and pushes hard on the pericarp. It breaks and the starch tissue inside is blown outward.
- The popping noise is the sound of steam escaping and the pericarp breaking.

## Fun Fact

The largest box of popcorn in the world was made in London in 2000. The box was 1.8 x 1.8 x 3.6 m (6 x 6 x 12 ft) and filled with 22.2 sq. m (784 sq. ft) of popcorn. It took five hours to fill.

## Mini Quiz

How did Ancient civilizations make popping corn pop?

## Mini Answer

In Peru, popcorn poppers date back to 300 A.D! The poppers were shallow vessels with a hole on the top and a single handle.

81

# Thirty Second Cloud

Clouds are made when air holding vapourised water cools. Try to make your own cloud inside a jar!

Rat's Rating

# What to do in this meteorology experiment

1  Pour a little water into the jar. Put the lid on tightly. Leave it for 20 minutes.

4  Cut off the neck of the balloon.

5  Take off the lid of the jar. Put in the chalk powder.

2  Put white chalk in a zip-lock bag. Zip the bag shut.

6  Quickly cover the jar with the balloon.

3  Use your hands to crush the chalk into a powder.

7 Put a rubber band around the neck of the jar to keep the balloon stretched tight.

RUBBER BAND

9 Take away the balloon. What do you see?

8 Press the balloon down with your fist to crush the air. Hold it like this for 30 seconds.

## What Happens
You have made a cloud.

## Why
- Cool air can't hold much water vapour. Some of it condenses to make clouds.
- When you compress the air in your jar, the air becomes warmer. It absorbs more vaporised water.
- When you take away the balloon cover, the air cools. Some of the vaporised water condenses on the chalk dust. It makes a cloud.

Here are the main four groups of clouds and their shapes: cumulus (heap), stratus (layer), cirrus (curl of hair) and nimbus (rain).

## Mini Quiz

Where does the expression 'on cloud nine' come from?

A CUMULUS cloud

A STRATUS cloud

A CIRRUS cloud

A NIMBUS cloud

A rather disagreeable cranky STORM cloud!

## Mini Answer

Being 'on cloud nine' means you are very happy. A famous Italian author, Dante, wrote a book about ten steps to heaven. Clouds were used as the steps. Cloud nine was as close to God as you could get.

# It's Just a Phase

Ever been told, 'You're just going through a phase'? Well, the moon goes through a phase, too. But it won't grow out of it.

I wonder if it is made out of green cheese... ...yum! Makes your mouth water.

**You will need:**
5 cm (2 in) or bigger white Styrofoam ball, lamp with a bright bulb (400 watts), sharp pencil

**Rat's Rating**

**Rat's Helpful Hint**
Make sure no one's head gets in the way of this experiment, or they will cause a lunar eclipse!

# What to do in this astronomy experiment

1   Put the lamp in the centre of the room.

2   Take away the lampshade. You only need to see the bulb.

3   Push the foam ball into the sharp end of the pencil.

4   Hold the pencil in your left hand.

5   Place the ball at arm's length between the bulb and your eyes. The bulb is the sun. The ball is the moon. You are the earth!

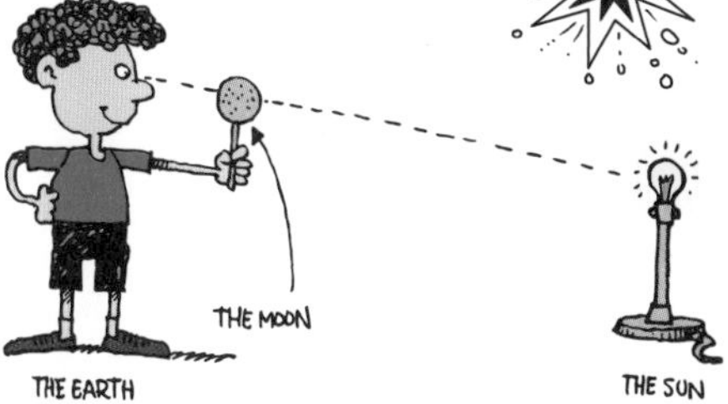

THE MOON

THE EARTH

THE SUN

6   Your ball (moon) is blocking the bulb (sun). This is what a total solar eclipse looks like!

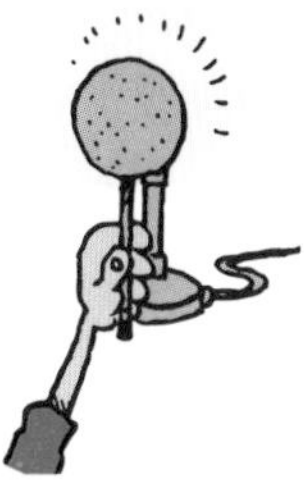

7  Move your ball (moon) so that you look into the bulb (sun). Look at your moon. All the light shines on the far side. This is opposite the side you are looking at. This phase is called the *new moon.*

8  Move your hand to the left, about 45 degrees of the way around counterclockwise. Look at the light on your moon. The right-hand edge is lit as a crescent. The crescent starts out very thin. It fattens up as the moon moves farther away from the sun.

9  When your moon is at 90 degrees to the left, the right half of the moon lights up.

10 Keep moving your hand counterclockwise. When the moon reaches directly opposite the sun, the part seen from earth is fully lit. Of course, only half of the moon is lit. It has taken the moon about two weeks to move from new to full.

11 Switch the pencil to your right hand. Face the lamp (sun).

12 Start with your moon at full. Keep going on its counterclockwise course. You'll see the opposite phases of the moon. The moon will reach the 270° position, straight out to the right. A thinning crescent and a return to new moon follows this.

270°

## What Happens

The moon chases the sun across the day and night sky.

## Why

- From full to new, the moon has been waning and leading the Sun.
- The phase cycle takes 29.53 days. Why not watch the real moon? Most newspapers give the moon phases along with the weather data.

# Micrometeorites

Has a meteor landed in your back yard? Try this experiment. You might be surprised.

**You will need:**
sheet of white paper, small paintbrush, jar, magnet, microscope

Rat's Rating

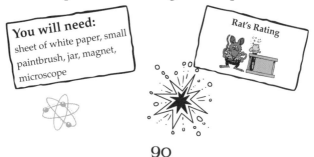

# What to do in this astronomy experiment

1   Find a place in your house where floating bits of fine particles collect. Window and door screens and the bottom of outside drain spouts work well.

2   Use a brush to collect the particles. Make sure they are dry and put them in a small jar.

3   Shake the particles onto a sheet of white paper. Roll the sides up. Gently tap all the particles into the centre of the sheet.

4   Place a magnet under the paper.

5   Gently tilt and tap the paper to get rid of non-magnetic particles. What is left?

## What Happens

Some of the left over metallic particles are bits of space dust! To look at them, place the paper under a microscope. You'll need to use high power to see them clearly. The micrometeorites will show signs of their fiery trip through the atmosphere. They will be rounded and may have small pits on their surfaces.

## Why

- Tons of space dust and debris blast the earth every day.
- Much of what you see are particles that date from when the solar system was formed.
- This is debris left from the raw materials that formed into the nine known planets and the asteroids. This was four to five billion years ago!
- Most particles have been broken off, or ground down from larger objects.

Shooting stars are not really stars. They are small bits of rock and metal that hit into the upper atmosphere of Earth. And, because of friction, burn up. Sometimes, man-made satellites and spacecraft parts fall into the atmosphere. These burn up the same way.

Well there goes the satellite broadcast of the big match.... because there goes the satellite through the Earth's atmosphere!

## Mini Quiz

Why are pieces of rock so important?

## Mini Answer

Meteorites are very important for scientists to study. Apart from a small amount of moon rock brought back by the *Apollo* and *Luna* missions, meteorites are the only material evidence that there is a universe beyond the Earth.

# Straw Oboe

Here is your chance to make all the noise you want –
and you can blame it all on science.

Rat's Rating

**You will need:**
drinking straw,
scissors

## Rat's Helpful Hint

Try this early on a Sunday morning
when the rest of the house is asleep.
The best way to do it is to stand by
a bedroom door. Be careful though,
sound bytes bite, so maybe you
really shouldn't!

# What to do in this astronomy experiment

**1** Pinch flat 12–19 mm (1/2 – 3/4 in) at one end of the straw.

**2** Cut off little triangles. These make the reeds.

**3** Put the straw far enough into your mouth so your lips do not touch the corners.

**4** Press with your lips on the straw, but not too hard. Blow gently just past the cut. Listen to the sound. Keep trying. It may take a few tries.

**5** Cut three small slits along the length of the straw about 2.5 cm (1 in) apart.

95

6 Separate the slits so they form small holes.

7 Cover one of them and blow as before.

8 Then cover two, then three, blowing each time. Keep listening.

## What Happens

Each time you blow, you hear a different sound. You can play simple tunes by covering and uncovering the holes.

## Why

- As in a real oboe, the reeds open and close at high speed.
- This first allows air to flow into the straw and then to stop the flow.
- Vibrating air makes the sound.
- As you cover and uncover the holes, you regulate the length of the air column. That decides the pitch.
- The shorter the air column, the faster it vibrates and the higher the note.

## Fun Fact

Another way to be heard is with a piece of cellophane 5 cm (2 in) square. Stretch it tightly between the thumbs and index fingers of both hands. Hold your hands in front of your face so the cellophane is in front of your lips. Blow hard and fast at the edge of the tightly stretched piece of cellophane. Keep your lips close together. You must send a thin stream of air right at the edge of the cellophane.

Can you hear a noise? When the air hits the edge of the cellophane, you'll make a scream. If you don't, change the distance between the cellophane and your lips until the air hits it just right. The fast-moving air from your lip makes the edges of the cellophane vibrate. Because the cellophane is very thin, the jet of air makes these vibrations very fast. The faster something vibrates, the higher the tone it creates.

## Mini Quiz

Which instrument sounds the 'tuning note' to which all the instruments of an orchestra, or band, adjust their tuning?

## Mini Answer

The oboe sounds the tuning note for the rest of an orchestra. It uses a double reed, which is two pieces of cane tied together.

Some parents proudly say their children play the violin . the trumpet .. or even . the drums! We have to say ours plays . THE CELLOPHANE !

EEEEEEEE
EEEEEEEE

# String Orchestra

String instruments make sounds with vibrating
strings. Let's see if you can too.

**You will need:**
two pieces of string,
paper cup, paperclips,
small can, water

Rat's Rating

# What to do in this sound experiment

1 Half fill the small can with water.

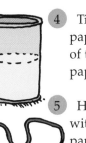

2 Tie one paperclip to the end of one piece of string.

3 Put the other string through the hole in the paper cup.

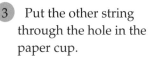

4 Tie the second paperclip to the end of the string in the paper cup.

5 Hold up the string without the cup, by the paperclip.

6 Wet your fingertips in the can of water.

7 Squeeze the string between your fingertips near the paperclip. Pull your fingers down the string. You should hear a sound.

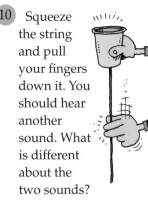

8 Hold up the cup with the string hanging down.

9 Get your fingers wet again.

10 Squeeze the string and pull your fingers down it. You should hear another sound. What is different about the two sounds?

## What Happens
The sound from the cup is louder.

## Why
- Vibrations in the string make the cup vibrate too.
- Since the cup is bigger, it moves more air. This makes a louder sound.
- The same thing happens with instruments like the violin. The vibrating strings make the wood body vibrate. This makes a louder sound.

The vibrating parts of musical instruments don't make sound waves of just one frequency. This is because the string, or forced air, doesn't just vibrate as a whole. Smaller parts also vibrate. In musical instruments, the extra frequencies are called *overtones*. When the overtones are close to the basic frequency, your brain thinks it's a single pitch (level of sound). Different instruments have different strengths of their overtones. This is also what makes your voice sound different from someone else's, even when you sing the exact same pitch.

## Mini Quiz

How do you measure sound?

OK...OK! Who's singing off key... as well as singing a different song from everyone else?

## Mini Answer

Sound is measured in decibels (dB) – this is the force of sound waves against the ear. The louder the sound, the more decibels it is. Here are approximate decibel levels for some everyday sounds:

Watch ticking 20
Normal talking 50
Doorbell 80
Baby crying 110
Sporting event 120
Kid's noisy squeeze toy 135
Rock concert 140
Jet engine taking off 150
Fireworks 160
Shotgun fire 170
Rocket launch 180

# The Bells! The Bells!

How can a spoon sound like a bell? No, this isn't a riddle. It's science!

**You will need:**
scissors, string, metal spoons (teaspoon, soup spoon, tablespoon/serving spoon)

Rat's Rating

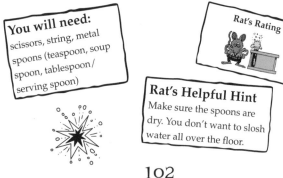

**Rat's Helpful Hint**
Make sure the spoons are dry. You don't want to slosh water all over the floor.

## What to do in this sound experiment

1. Cut a piece of string into a 75 cm (30 in) length.

2. Tie a loop in the middle of the string, but don't pull it into a knot.

3. Put the handle of the teaspoon through the loop. Pull the loop tight so the spoon won't slip out.

4. Move the spoon so that it hangs with the round end just a little lower than the handle.

5. Press one end of the string against the outside of your right ear.

6. Press the other end against the outside of your left ear.

7. Swing the string gently so the curve of the spoon hits the edge of a table. What do you hear?

## What Happens

By swinging the spoon gently, you'll hear a bell ring! Repeat the experiment by using a soup spoon and listen to the difference in sound. Now try a tablespoon or serving spoon. The bigger the size, the deeper the sound.

This must surely be BIG BEN

## Why

- The metal in the spoon starts to vibrate when it hits the table.
- The string conducts this vibration.
- The molecules in the spoon move back and forth (vibrate), and hit against each other.
- When molecules hit, energy moves from one molecule to the other.
- The vibrating molecules in the spoon hit against the molecules of the string.
- Not only does string carry sound waves better than air, it sends them right into your ear. This is why you hear the deep sound of bells.

Indian snake charmers don't play old-fashioned traditional tunes to charm their snakes. Instead, they play popular music from current Indian films!

I'm not even thinking of coming out until you put on the theme from the movie... 'SHE BROKE MY HEART OVER A DISH OF TANDOORI ONE NIGHT IN THE PUNJAB'

## Mini Quiz

How do you hear sound?

## Mini Answer

You hear sound because of movement in the air. As the source of a sound vibrates, it moves the air molecules around. These in turn set air molecules around them vibrating, and so the sound is sent through the air to your ears. When the air molecules in your ear start vibrating, your eardrum vibrates. It passes the movement to the inner ear. Nerves then take the information to the brain and you hear sound.

# It's Snot Fair!

Feel left out when your friends are fussed over because they have colds and you don't? Try making your own mucus! It looks just as revolting as the real stuff, but you don't have to get sick.

AARR-CHOO! Oh I've got a terrible cold!!

Only joking! ...it's just another experiment!

Rat's Rating

**You will need:**
corn syrup/golden syrup, unflavoured gelatin, measuring cup, water, microwave oven or stove, green food colouring (optional but it makes the mix look disgusting), fork

## What to do in this anatomy experiment

1 Ask an adult to help you heat 1/2 cup of water until it boils.

2 Take the pan off the heat. Add a tiny drop of food colouring to the water.

3 Sprinkle in three envelopes of unflavoured gelatin.

4 Let it soften a few minutes and stir with a fork.

5 Add enough corn syrup to make 1 cup of the thick mixture.

URRR!
Where's
my
hanky?

6 Stir with a fork and lift out the long strands of gunk.

7 As it cools, you'll need to add more water, spoonful by spoonful.

## What Happens
You have made fake or artificial mucus.

## Why
- Mucus is mainly made out of sugars and protein. That is what you used to make your fake mucus, only you use different proteins and different sugars.
- Those long, fine strings inside your fake mucus are proteins. They are why real mucus can stretch out quite long.
- The protein helps make it sticky, too. The protein in your fake mucus is gelatin.

## Fun Fact

Put a pinch of fine dust onto your fake mucus. Now stir it up. Look closely into the goo from the side. The fine dust is trapped. That is why you have mucus in your nose. You use it to trap all the dust, pollen and junk that is floating in the air. With mucus, most of the dirt is trapped and then blown out.

You wouldn't want to see what's in this hankerchief... IT'S THE REAL THING!

## Mini Answer

The reason your stomach is not destroyed by acid is thanks to mucus. Mucus is thick, sticky, slimy and gooey, and the inside of your stomach is covered with it. That layer of mucus protects the stomach from its own acid. Your stomach has to make a new layer of mucus every two weeks otherwise it will digest itself.

## Mini Quiz

Your stomach has *hydrochloric acid* inside. This acid is strong enough to eat through a piece of the metal zinc. Why doesn't this eat through you and make you melt?

# Print Those Fingers

I'd say they were RAT PRINTS! LAB RAT to be precise!

Have a look at the tip of your fingers. Look at the grooves in your skin. They make a pattern called a fingerprint. Why not see what your print looks like?

**You will need:**
ink, inkpad or pencil, sheet of white paper, clear tape, magnifying glass

Rat's Rating

## What to do in this anatomy experiment (using ink)

1 Pour a small amount of ink onto an inkpad. You can also use a saucer with a piece of sponge.

2 Dip your finger into the ink.

3 Lift your finger out.

4 Carefully press your inky finger onto a sheet of white paper.

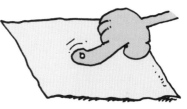

## What to do (using pencil)

1 Using a sharp pencil, rub the end across a sheet of paper until you get a layer of *graphite* on the paper.

111

2 Rub your finger across the graphite on the paper.

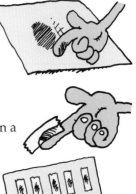

3 Tear off about 2.5 cm (1 in) of clear tape and stick it across the dark end of your finger.

4 Remove the tape and stick it on a sheet of white paper.

5 Repeat the process until all your fingers are fingerprinted. Have a close look at each pattern through a magnifying glass.

## What Happens

The pattern on each fingerprint is the same.

## Why

- The inner layer of skin is the *dermis*. It has projections.
- The outer layer is the *epidermis*. It fits over these projections and takes on the same pattern.
- These projections are made five months before a baby is born! They never change.

## Fun Fact

Fingerprints are very useful for telling who people are. This is because no two people in the world have the same fingerprint. When police try to solve a crime, they use fingerprinting. This means they can see who was at the scene of the crime. They can check these prints with the fingerprints of a suspect.

What sort of thief would play with a stamp pad before he does a job?

One who wants to get caught obviously!

## Mini Quiz

Do animals have fingerprints?

## Mini Answer

Yes, many animals have their own type of fingerprints. The dorsal fins and saddle patches of orcas (whales) are unique to each individual. No two lions have the same pattern of whiskers. No two tigers or zebras have the same pattern of stripes. The fingerprints of koalas are so close to those of humans, that they could be confused at a crime scene!

113

# 'Eye' Can See Better Than You

How do animals see the world? Here's your chance to find out. It is a real eye-opener!

Will you look at that! If I look like... THIS... I can see like a RAT!

Rat's Rating

## What to do in this zoology experiment (a)

1  Cut a piece of shiny card 30 cm (12 in) long and 9 cm (3.5 in) wide.

2  Cut an arch about halfway on the card to fit your nose.

3  Put the card to your face. Your nose must fit in the arch, and the card must touch your forehead.

4  Bend the sides of the card slightly away from your head.

5  Flex the ends of the card so what you see is clearly in focus.

6  What is different about the way you now see things?

## What Happens
You can see from either side of your head at the same time!

## What to do (b)

1 Cut two egg holders from the carton.

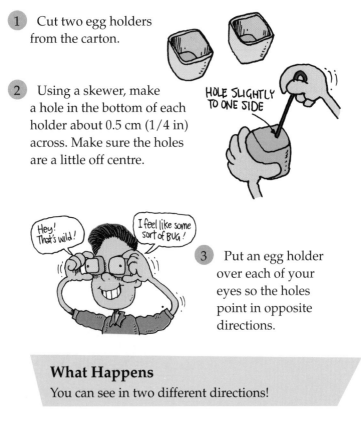

2 Using a skewer, make a hole in the bottom of each holder about 0.5 cm (1/4 in) across. Make sure the holes are a little off centre.

HOLE SLIGHTLY TO ONE SIDE

Hey! That's wild!

I feel like some sort of BUG!

3 Put an egg holder over each of your eyes so the holes point in opposite directions.

## What Happens

You can see in two different directions!

## Why

- The position of an animal's eyes changed over time to suit its needs.
- Our eyes are placed up front. This gives us *binocular* vision and depth perception. This was vital for an animal that once swung through the trees.
- Animals like horses and rabbits have eyes high and to the sides of their head. This lets them see nearly 360 degrees, as well as far above their head. They have a small blind spot directly in front of their face, but forward placed nostrils and big ears make up for that.
- Chameleons see in different directions at the same time. This way they can watch for danger out of one eye and search for food with the other.

Well...I've had quite enough of that program thankyou...I'll be up all night with nightmares!

### Fun Fact

A television screen shows 24 pictures each second. Because a fly sees 200 images each second, a fly watching television sees it as still pictures with darkness in-between. For a fly's eye view, try to flicker your eyelids very fast.

### Mini Quiz

How far can an eagle see?

### Mini Answer

An eagle can see a rabbit from about 1.6 km (1 mi) away.

117

# Brain Pattern

Are you good at concentrating? I think you'd better
try this experiment.

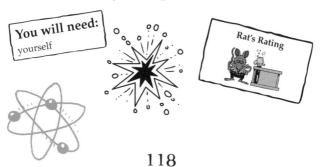

You will need:
yourself

Rat's Rating

## What to do in this anatomy experiment

1 Pat the top of your head with one hand.

2 At the same time, pat your stomach with your other hand.

3 Keep patting your head, but start to rub your stomach in a circle movement.

4 Swap over. Now, rub your head while patting your stomach.

119

## What Happens

It is easy for the hands to do the same pattern of movement. But it is hard to do two different movements at the same time.

## Why

- When you repeat the same movement, you get used to moving your hands in the same pattern. Your brain is programmed to do this.
- Back and forth movements or circular patterns are easy to do, but only one pattern at a time. Both types of movement are programmed into the brain.
- It takes much more concentration to do two programs at the same time.

## Fun Fact

Your brain has a special clock inside. It tells you when to sleep and when to wake up. Without it you'd be waking and sleeping all through the day. The clock is an actual cluster of *neurons*. These send nerve impulses to the brain. The impulses tell us that it is time to go to bed and eight hours later they tell us to wake up.

TICK TICK
TICK TICK
TICK TICK TICK
TICK
TICK

It sounds like someone's brain is ticking!

## Mini Quiz

If you have a big brain, are you more intelligent than someone with a small brain?

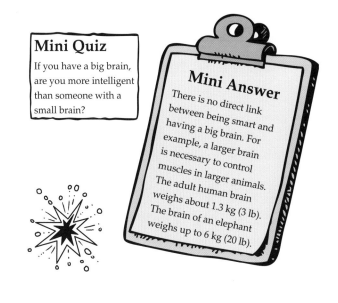

## Mini Answer

There is no direct link between being smart and having a big brain. For example, a larger brain is necessary to control muscles in larger animals. The adult human brain weighs about 1.3 kg (3 lb). The brain of an elephant weighs up to 6 kg (20 lb).

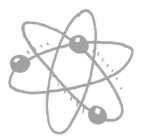

# Check Your Pulse is True Not False

Your heart beats about 100,000 times in one day and about 35 million times in a year. During your life, it will beat more than 2.5 billion times! Want to check if yours is still going?

**You will need:**
yourself, clock or watch with a second hand

Rat's Rating

## What to do in this anatomy experiment

**1**  Take two fingers, the second and
third finger work best, and place
them in the groove in the wrist that
lies under the thumb.

**2**  Move your fingers back and forth
gently. What can you feel?

**3**  Take the
same two
fingers and
run them
alongside the
outer edge of
your wind-
pipe. What can
you feel this
time? In both
cases, you will
feel a slight
throb. Do you know why this is?

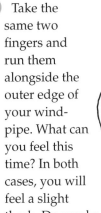

TRY
HERE

## What Happens

The throb you feel is your pulse. It throbs as blood moves through your arteries. The first pulse is that of the *radial artery*. It takes blood to the hand. The second pulse is that of the *carotid artery*. It takes blood to the brain, head and neck. Count the throbs. How many do you count in 15 seconds? Time yourself, or have someone count 15 seconds for you. Multiply your total by 4 and you'll know your pulse rate in beats per minute. Your resting pulse will range from 90–120 beats per minute. An adult has a pulse of about 72 beats a minute. Hummingbirds have an average heart rate of 1,260 beats a minute!

## Why

- The pulse represents the beating of the heart.
- As your heart contracts, blood is forced through your blood vessels.
- The blood moves at a rhythmic rate based on your heartbeat.
- This causes the blood vessels in your wrist and neck, and other spots, to pulsate.
- All blood vessels have this throbbing movement.
- The vessels in the wrist are close to the surface of the skin. They are felt more easily.

You can watch your heart beat. Dim the lights. Lie on your back with your feet pointing towards a wall. Turn on the flashlight. Put it on your chest with the light end resting on the upper, left side of your chest and the beam shining on the wall by your feet. As you watch the beam, it will move up and down as your heart beats.

Want to speed up your heart a bit? Stand up and run on the spot for a minute. Lie down again and put the flashlight back in place. Do you notice a difference? Exercise means that your muscles need more oxygen. Your heart must pump more blood through your lungs, and then pump it out to your muscles. Your heart beats faster and harder, to pump more blood. If you keep watching, you'll see your heart rate slow down as your body catches up on its supply of oxygen.

## Mini Quiz

How much blood does your body have?

What's that terrible THUMPING noise?

Just my old ticker! I've just run a marathon!!

THUMPA
THUMPA
THUMPA
THUMPA

## Mini Answer

Your body has about 5.6 litres (6 quarts) of blood. The blood travels through your body three times every minute. In one day, the blood travels a total of 19,000 km (12,000 mi). That's four times the distance across America from coast to coast.

# Water Wall

A *tsunami* (soo-nam-ee) is the Japanese word for 'harbour wave'. It's a series of travelling waves made by an earthquake below the ocean floor. The waves may even have enough energy to travel across a whole ocean. Tsunamis get higher when they near shallow water.
See if you can make your own water wall.

Rat's Rating

**You will need:**
deep baking pan, water, blocks of wood

**Rat's Helpful Hint**
Want to see an adult explode? No? Then you better do it outside and on a warm day.

126

# What to do in this forces experiment

1 Fill the pan with water.

2 Place two blocks of
wood in the bottom
of the pan. They
must be completely
below the surface of
the water.

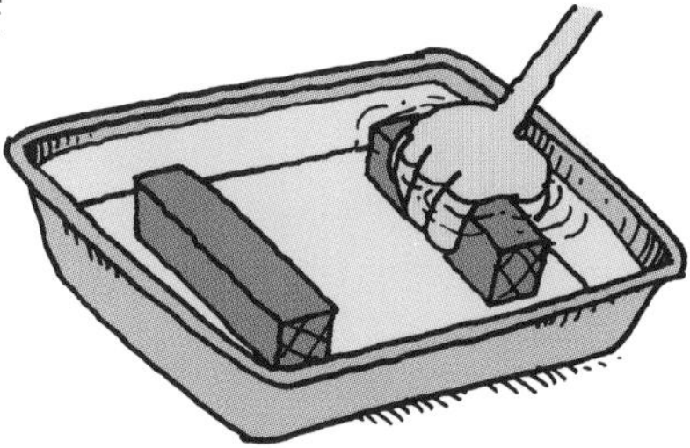

3 Hold the blocks
and quickly bring
them together.

4 Do it again and
again.

5 Continue the
squeezing action
until the blocks
can no longer squeeze the water.

## What Happens

The movement of the blocks coming together quickly under the water forces swells of water to the surface. These make waves that splash over the sides of the pan.

## Why

- The action of the blocks and the water is like the conditions in the ocean that make a tsunami.
- On the ocean floor, earthquakes and volcanic eruptions affect the water. They squeeze together large volumes of water and push it to the surface.
- On the surface they make great walls of water.

## Fun Fact

It is hard to see tsunamis travel through the ocean. This is because they may be only 30 cm (12 in) high. This changes when the wave nears the shore. The waves can reach heights of 15 to 30 m (50 to 100 ft). The largest recorded tsunami measured 64 m (210 ft) above sea level. That is as high as an 18-storey building! It reached Siberia's Kamchatka Peninsula in 1737.

## Mini Quiz

How fast can a tsunami travel?

## Mini Answer

A tsunami can move as fast as 804 km (500 mi) per hour.

129

# Hubble Bubble

Bubbles are a great way to explore science. Let's see how.

This experiment started off as me washing my coffee cup

Rat's Rating

## You will need:
plastic cup, bubble blower, bubble mix (store bought or homemade), plastic drinking straw, loop of wire made from a coat hanger or pipe cleaner

## Rat's Helpful Hint
Bubble mix is easy to make from dishwashing liquid. Make sure an adult is supervising. Gently mix 1 part detergent to 8–10 parts of warm water. For example, 1 tablespoon (15 ml) of detergent for every 1/2 cup (125 ml) of water. More detergent than water makes bigger bubbles. Your bubbles will last longer if you let the mix stand for one to two days before use. With store bought bubble mix, put it in the refrigerator for a few minutes before using it.

## What to do in this water experiment

1. Turn the plastic cup upside down.

2. Wet the bottom of the cup, which is now on top.

4. Wet the plastic straw in the bubble mix.

3. Use the wire loop to make a large bubble. Attach it to the wet plastic cup.

5. Gently push it through the large bubble.

6. Blow a smaller bubble inside the large one.

7 Carefully push the straw through the smaller bubble and blow an even smaller bubble.

## What Happens
You get a bubble in a bubble in a bubble.

## Why
- Bubbles are bits of air or gas trapped inside a liquid ball.
- The surface of a bubble is very thin.
- Bubbles are very fragile when a dry object touches them. That is because soap film sticks to the object, which puts a strain on the bubble.
- Anything wet can enter the bubble without breaking it.
- The wet surface meeting the soapy film becomes part of it.
- If you want your bubbles to last longer, keep everything wet, even the sides of the straw. Don't touch the wet wall with your smaller bubble. If you do, you won't get a separate bubble.

## Mini Quiz

What have bubbles got in common with honeycomb?

15 seconds after the WORLD'S BIGGEST BUBBLE GUM BUBBLE RECORD was blown

## Mini Answer

Get two sheets of clear plastic. Separate them by a finger and soak them in soapy water. Then blow bubbles between the sheets. You'll get many bubble walls. If your bubbles are of the same size, you'll see that they make hexagons and look like the cells of a beehive. Bees, like bubbles, try to be as efficient as possible when making the comb. They want to use the minimum possible amount of wax to get the job done.

# Moving Water

**Rat's Rating**

This water is going to move.... I just haven't worked out how yet? That's the EXPERIMENT

**Do hot and cold water mix?**

**You will need:**
clear jars the same size (baby food jars work well), food colouring (red and blue look good), card to fit over the mouth of your jar, water, sink.

## What to do in this water experiment

1   Pour cold water and a few drops of blue colouring into jar 1. Slowly add more water until you see a bulge of water over the rim of the jar.

2   Ask an adult to boil some water. Have them fill jar 2 with hot water.

③ Put a few drops of red food colouring into jar 2.

④ Lay the card carefully on the top of jar 1.

⑤ This part is tricky. You may want to do it over a sink! Pick up jar 1. Turn it upside down. Put it over jar 2. You want the card to be flat and make a seal. You don't need to put your hand on the card. The water will hold it in place. Just flip the jar over. Don't stop for a

second! If the jar tilts, but isn't turned over completely, the water will gush out.

⑥ Keep the necks of the jars close together. Ask an adult to hold onto both jars while you very slowly and carefully pull out the card. What happens? What colour is the cold water in the top jar? What colour is the hot water in the bottom jar?

(7) Empty both jars. Rinse them. Repeat steps 1 through to 6, but put the jar with the cold water in the sink and put the card on top of the jar with the red-coloured hot water. Turn the hot water jar upside down and put it on top of the cold water jar. What happens? What colour is the water in the top jar? What colour is the water in the bottom jar?

HOT
(RED)
RISES
INTO THE
BLUE

## What Happens

The red-coloured hot water rises into the cold water jar.

## Why

- Cold water is heavier than hot water.
- The cold water goes down into the bottom jar pushing the hot water up in small currents.
- When you heat water, the water molecules start moving around faster and faster. They bounce off each other and move further apart.
- Because there is more space between the molecules, a volume of hot water has fewer molecules in it. It weighs a bit less than the same volume of cold water. So hot water is less dense than cold water.
- When you put the two jars together with the hot water on the bottom, the hot water rises to the top.
- Along the way, it mixes with the cold water and makes purple water.
- When the cold water is on the bottom, the water does not mix. The hot water does not have to rise – it is already on top!

Would you spend $100 for a glass of water? In America around 1848, people on the way west to the California gold rush did. Because of poor planning, many people weren't ready for the hot, dry deserts of Nevada. A few men in California knew this and travelled east with barrels of water. Very thirsty people paid up to $100 for a glass of precious water.

## Mini Quiz

Which Australian animal doesn't drink water?

## Mini Answer

The koala! The name koala comes from the native Australian word for 'no drink'. Koalas get the water they need from eating eucalyptus leaves.

# Baked Ice Cream

**Have you ever wondered how ice cream can be baked without melting? Try it and see.**

## You will need:
eggs, cream of tartar, salt, vanilla essence/extract, measuring spoons, castor/fine sugar, packet of big biscuits (chocolate chip are good!), ice cream, oven, baking tray, parchment paper, ice-cream scoop, egg whisk, bowl

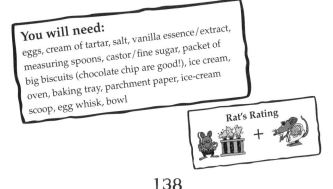

Rat's Rating

## What to do in this chemistry experiment

1. You will need adult supervision. Let three eggs come to room temperature.

2. Separate the whites of the eggs from the yolks.

3. Put the egg whites in a bowl.

4. Add 1/4 teaspoon cream of tartar, 1/4 teaspoon salt and 1/2 teaspoon vanilla extract.

5. Whisk the mixture until it stands up in stiff peaks.

6. Slowly add 1 cup of sugar by sprinkling a tablespoon at a time over the mixture.

7. Continue to stir until the meringue mixture is thick and glossy.

8. Cover the baking tray with parchment paper.

9. Put the biscuits on the baking tray. Leave gaps between them.

10 Place a small scoop of ice cream on each biscuit. Keep the ice cream away from the edges of the biscuits.

11 Spoon the meringue mixture over the ice cream. You must make sure the ice cream is completely covered by the meringue.

MERINGUE

ICE CREAM

12 Ask an adult to bake the meringues on the bottom rack of a cool oven at 110°C (230°F) for about 1 hour. Make sure the meringues don't get brown.

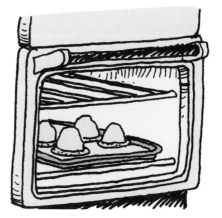

## What Happens

The warm oven cooks the meringues, but the ice cream doesn't melt!

ICE CREAM

## Why

- Cream of tartar is an acid. When it becomes moist, it releases carbon dioxide. This helps to aerate the meringue.
- When egg whites are beaten, they too make small air spaces.
- Both the air and carbon dioxide are trapped in the beaten egg white. They act as an insulator. As the sugar cooks it hardens. It also acts as an insulator.
- Insulation has small air spaces trapped in it. These slow the movement of heat or cold.
- When the meringue is spread over ice cream, the ice cream is insulated. The heat of the oven can't get in during the baking. Insulation lets the meringue cook without melting the ice cream.

141

# Smarty-pants

Are colours just one colour?
Or are they a mixture of separate colours?
Let's use confectionery to see how chromatography works.

**You will need:**
white coffee filter paper/white paper towels, bag of multi-coloured chocolate buttons, water, plate, scissors

Rat's Rating

## What to do in this physics experiment

1. Cut the paper filters into circles about 15 cm (6 in) across.

2. Place the plate on a flat surface. Lay the paper on the plate.

3. Place a coated chocolate button in the centre of the paper.

4. Dip your finger into the water. Hold it above the coated chocolate button. Let enough water drip onto the confectionery so that the water starts going onto the paper.

5. Repeat slowly until the confectionery is very wet and the circle of water on the paper towel is about 5 cm (2 in) across.

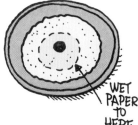

WET PAPER TO HERE

6. Leave for a while, but keep checking. Something is going to happen.

143

## What Happens

Rings of colour form around the confectionery. Repeat with different colours – which one is made of the most different inks? Now, eat it! Once the shell is wet, what do you notice about the candy? It's not so crispy, is it?

## Why

- The colour in the sugar coating of the confectionery shell dissolves in the water.
- The water is drawn out through the paper by capillary action. It moves in a growing circle.
- The different inks that make up the colour of the confectionery move at different speeds and so they are separated.
- At the molecular level, smaller hydrophilic (a substance that loves water) molecules move faster through the paper.
- The colours that move the furthest from the confectionery have less of a mass than the ones closest.

## Fun Fact

We usually think of water running downhill, but capillary action makes water go up! Want to see how? Get a celery stalk. Put it in a jar with water and food colouring. The next day look at the celery. Cut the stalk and see how far up the stalk the coloured water travelled. Try the same thing with a white flower such as a carnation, daisy or chrysanthemum. How long does it take before the white petals change colour?

Alfonse...I'm in one of those happy-go-lucky kind of moods. What colour do you suggest?

I'd go for sticking you in a jar of 'VIVID ORANGE'

## Mini Quiz

Where did the idea for M&M's® come from?

## Mini Answer

The idea for M&M's® came from the Spanish Civil War! The story is that on a trip to Spain, Forrest Mars Sr met soldiers who were eating pellets of chocolate in a hard sugary coating. The coating stopped the chocolate from melting. Mr. Mars went back to his kitchen and invented the recipe for M&M's®. They were first sold to the public in 1941 and were popular with American soldiers serving in World War II.

145

# Iron for Breakfast

Feeling hungry? Would you eat an iron nail?
Most enriched breakfast cereals add metallic iron
as a health supplement. Try this experiment.

**You will need:**
two different breakfast cereals (one
healthy, one not!), bowls, pencil,
magnets, zip-lock plastic bags, tape,
water, white coffee filters/paper towels,
microscope or magnifying glass

Rat's Rating

# What to do in this chemistry experiment

**1**  Put 1/2 cup of each cereal into two separate zip-lock bags. Zip up the bags.

**4**  Add 1 cup of water to each bowl and stir. If needed, use extra water to keep the mixture thin and soupy.

**2**  Use your hands to crush the cereal to a fine powder.

**5**  Tape a small magnet to the eraser end of a pencil. Seal it inside a plastic bag.

**3**  Pour each crushed cereal into a different bowl.

6  Stir the cereal mix
   with the magnet for
   10 minutes.

7  Lift out the magnet.
   What do you see? Gently
   wipe the magnet on the
   filter paper.

## What Happens

Small bits of pure iron filings have collected on
the magnet! The filings will look like small dark
dots on the magnet. Sometimes they'll clump
together. If you have trouble seeing the filings,
try looking through a microscope or magnifying
glass.

IRON
FILINGS

## Why

- Magnets attract iron.
- Magnets will stick to anything
  that has iron in it.
- Our bodies don't have very
  much iron, so magnets don't
  stick to us.

148

The human body needs iron for many functions. Most importantly, iron is used to make *haemoglobin* in red blood cells. It is the iron in the haemoglobin that attracts oxygen molecules. This lets the blood cells carry oxygen to other cells in the body. Red blood cells are always being replaced. This is why your diet needs a constant supply of iron. Iron is put in some foods and vitamin pills as a healthy additive.

A little too much of that IRON-enriched breakfast cereal

## Mini Quiz

Is the iron in cereals the same iron as found in nails, cars and machinery?

## Mini Answer

Yes! The iron in cereal is pure iron! Really! It's mixed in the cereal batter along with other additives. The tiny particles of iron quickly react with hydrochloric acid and other chemicals in the digestive tract. This changes them into a form easily absorbed by the body.

# The Invisible Shield

Rat's Rating

I wish this rain would stop so I could use my INVISIBLE SHIELD to deflect incoming missiles or bad guys...and not just rain.

**Is air strong? Can it protect you? Air is all around you, but do you pay any attention to it? Can something you can't see, like air, protect something you can see, like a newspaper?**

## Rat's Helpful Hint
Don't use the newspaper before your parents have read the sports page and cut out recipes from the lifestyle section. Shredded newspaper from your pet's cage or litter tray will not work!

## You will need:
newspaper, small empty glass, bowl of cold water, a rainy day (optional)

## What to do in this forces experiment

1 Stand in the rain. Put half a sheet of newspaper over your head. Does the paper stop you from getting wet? No, the water soaks into the paper, doesn't it?

2 Get another dry half sheet of newspaper.

3 Push the newspaper into the glass. It must be pushed in tightly. Make sure the newspaper is clear of the rim.

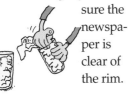

4 Turn the glass upside down.

5 Sink the glass into a bowl of water. The rim of the glass must rest on the bottom of the bowl.

6 Hold the glass there. Count to 10.

7 Take the glass straight out of the water. Wipe the rim.

8 Turn the glass the right side up. Do you think the newspaper will be wet or dry?

9 Take out the newspaper and see.

151

## What Happens

The newspaper is dry!

## Why

- Air molecules are invisible. But they still have weight, so they take up space.
- Water can't get into the glass because the glass is actually full of air molecules.
- When the glass is pushed into the water, the molecules don't escape. Instead, they are pressed together.
- The air can't get out because it is lighter than water. The air acts as a shield between the water and the newspaper. Some water may enter the glass, but not enough to wet the paper.

Air pressure can tell us what kind of weather to expect. A high pressure system usually means clear skies. If a low pressure system is coming, then look for storms and rain.

A rather large LOW PRESSURE SYSTEM moved in between the bus stop and our front door catching me off guard dear!

## Mini Quiz

Earth's atmosphere presses against every part of you. It does this with a force of 1 kg per square cm (14.7 pounds per square inch). Over 1,000 square cm (1 square foot) the force is almost one ton! What stops air pressure from squashing you?

## Mini Answer

The air molecules inside your body stop you from being squashed. The air inside you balances the pressure outside. This keeps you firm and not squishy. The next time someone says that they are 'under pressure' you'd better agree with them.

153

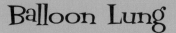

# Balloon Lung

Another Birthday Party! That means BALLOON LUNG!

**What does your lung look like when it breathes air? Find out!**

Rat's Rating

## Rat's Helpful Hint

Make sure the bottle has your favourite drink. That way you'll get a chance to drink it all before you start the experiment.

## You will need:

clear plastic bottle, balloon, plastic funnel

154

## What to do in this anatomy experiment

1. Blow up and let out the air in a balloon 10 times. This makes it soft and baggy.

2. Push the balloon 1 cm (1/2 in) over the neck of a funnel about 14 cm (5 in) wide.

3. Push the balloon and neck of the funnel into a clear plastic bottle. The balloon should partly inflate.

4. Squeeze the sides of the bottle and let go of your grip 10 times. What does the balloon do?

breathe out

155

breathe in

## What Happens
The balloon is breathing just like a real lung.

## Why
- The air is forced out of the balloon.
- When you release your grip, the balloon fills again.
- When you breathe in, the muscles in your chest cavity contract and expand.
- This makes the pressure in the chest cavity lower than the outside air pressure.
- Air then flows in through the airways and inflates the lungs.
- When you breathe out, your muscles relax. Your chest cavity gets smaller.
- The decrease in volume of the cavity increases the pressure in the chest cavity above the outside air pressure.
- Air from the lungs (high pressure) then flows out of the airways to the outside air (low pressure). The cycle then repeats with each breath.

What if every tree in the forest breathed out at the same time!

## Mini Quiz

Which part of your body has a surface area about the same size as a tennis court?

## Mini Answer

Your lungs.

# I Can. Can You?

Things don't always act as you expect when you put them under pressure.

**You will need:**
empty aluminium soft drink can, big bowl, a pair of kitchen tongs

Rat's Rating

# What to do in this forces experiment

1. Fill the bowl with cold water.

2. Put 1 tablespoon of water into the empty can.

3. Ask an adult to heat the can over a stove to boil the water. Use the tongs to hold the can.

4. When the water boils watch the can. A cloud of condensed vapour will escape from the hole. Let the water boil for about 30 seconds.

5. Quickly turn the can upside down and dip it into the water in the bowl. Does the water in the bowl flow into the hole in the can? Or does something else happen?

## What Happens

Bang! The can will collapse almost immediately. Some water from the pan may get into the can, but not fast enough to fill the can before the air outside crushes it.

## Why

- When you heat the can you make the water boil.
- The vapour from the boiling water pushes the cool air out of the can.
- When the can is filled with water vapour, it is cooled suddenly when turned upside down in the water.
- Cooling the can condenses the water vapour inside the can.
- This leaves less air in the can than there was originally. When this happens, the pressure of the air outside the can is greater than the pressure inside. This causes the air outside to crush the can.

## Fun Fact

You can crush an open aluminium can with your hand. When you squeeze the can, the pressure outside becomes greater than the pressure inside. If you squeeze hard enough, the can collapses.

I think the idea is to drink what's in the can before you crush it.

CRUNCH

## Mini Quiz

How long does it take an aluminium can to decompose?

## Mini Answer

It takes over 500 years for an aluminium can to decompose.

# Magical Marbles

I would have been the wizard of the rat hole as a kid if I'd had these!

ABRACADABRA

MAGIC MARBLES

Inertia is the way a body will stay still, or move, unless acted upon by an external force.
Want to see how it works?
You'll have to move your body then!

**You will need:**
two rulers, marbles, tape

Rat's Rating

## What to do in this physics experiment

1. Tape the rulers to a flat surface. They need to be parallel and about 1.5 cm (1/2 in) apart.

2. Put two marbles in the middle of the rulers 5 cm (a few inches) apart

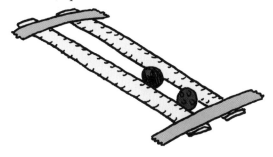

3. Gently tap one marble so it rolls and hits the second one. What happens?

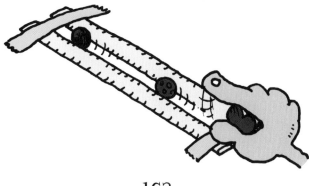

## What Happens

The marble that had been rolling stops. And the one that had been still, now rolls! The force of the rolling marble transfers to the other one. It stops the first and sets the second in motion. Now put two marbles on the stick so they touch and a third marble several centimetres (a few inches) away. Gently tap the single marble into the other two. Notice that the rolling marble stops, the middle one stays still and the third one rolls! The momentum went through the second marble into the third! Try other combinations, two marbles into three still marbles, or three into three. You will find that however many marbles you set in motion, the same number will be made to roll when they are hit.

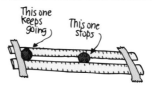

## Why

- Inertia is the way one object sets another object in motion.
- An object at rest tends to stay at rest. An object that is moving tends to keep moving in the same direction.
- An object stays at rest, or keeps moving, unless some external force acts upon it.

Can a paper straw go through a raw potato? Here is another inertia activity. Put a potato on the kitchen bench. If the potato is old, soak it in water for 30 minutes first. Hold it firmly with one hand. Make sure your hand is not underneath the potato. With a fast, strong push, stab the potato with the straw. The straw pierces the potato without bending or buckling.

People go to all the trouble to get a straw into a potato.... But then what are you supposed to do with it?

Suck out the juice?

## Mini Quiz

How can something as soft as a stalk of grain go through a wall?

## Mini Answer

Inertia causes stalks in fields to go into and through wooden barns and houses when propelled by tornado force winds at least 177 km/h (110 mph).

# Am I Attractive?

Magnets are more human than you think.
Their poles can attract each other as well
as repel each other.

Rat's Rating

**Rat's Helpful Hint**
Just remember to keep your magnet
away from audio and videotapes and
computer disks, or you might erase
the information on them!

**You will need:**
modelling clay, sharp
pencil with an eraser,
horseshoe magnet

## What to do in this magnet experiment

1. Roll the piece of clay into a ball.

3. Push the eraser end of the pencil into the clay.

2. Flatten it to make a cone shape.

4. Carefully balance the horseshoe magnet on the pencil lead.

## What Happens

The magnet slowly moves itself into a north-south direction.

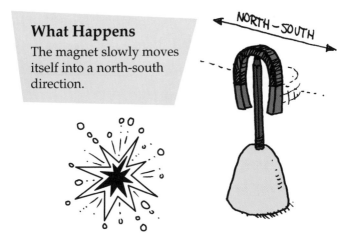

## Why

- The earth has a magnetic field, which isn't very strong, but it's enough to attract your magnet. The magnet turned in a north-south direction.
- Five billion years ago, the earth was made in a big mix of meteorites and comets. The huge amount of heat melted the planet. It's still cooling off today!
- Denser materials like iron from the meteorites sank to create the core of the earth. As it rotated, it made a magnetic field.

## Fun Fact

Cows like to graze on grass. Unfortunately, bolts, nails and bits of barbed wire end up in the grass. The cows eat these by mistake. Some cows have even died when trying to pass them through their digestive system. To solve the problem, farmers can feed calves magnets! The magnets stay in the cow's stomachs their whole life and hold onto the metal. This means the metal doesn't go through their digestive systems.

She calls it.. 'a magnetic personality'. But I think there's something else going on there!

## Mini Quiz

Imagine that you are in the middle of the ocean. All you see is water and it is a cloudy day so you cannot see the sun. How would you know which way to go?

## Mini Answer

No matter where you are on earth, you can hold a compass and it will point toward the North Pole. Long before space satellites and other high-tech navigational aids, a compass was the best way to know which way to go.

# You Smell!

**Want to find out more?**

**You will need:**
a friend, blindfold, item of clothing from each member of your family

Rat's Rating

# What to do in this biology experiment

1 Put on the blindfold. Don't peek.

2 Ask your friend to get an item of clothing that someone has just taken off. Hopefully not smelly socks! Have something from each member of your family.

3 Get your friend to hold the clothing under your nose. But don't touch it.

4 Concentrate and tell whose clothing it is just by the smell.

## What Happens

You should be able to tell which item of clothing belongs to each family member.

## Why

- The smell comes from the *pheromones* our body makes.
- We all have own special smell. The smell is ours alone and different from anyone else.
- We get used to these smells and don't notice them.
- Our smells even change the fragrance of perfume or cologne. That's why these are a little different on every person. It's also the reason different houses smell differently.

172

Be careful not to squash a wasp near its nest. A dying wasp gives out an alarm pheromone. This calls other wasps to come and help. Within 15 seconds, wasps within a 4.5 m (15 ft) area will attack you for squashing their friend!

## Mini Quiz

Why do feet often smell so bad?

## Mini Answer

Very tiny plants and animals grow on your skin and inside you. Gross! But true!

These microbes make your feet smell bad because, as they grow, they're smelly. We can wash some of them off, but microbes duplicate, so we can never get rid of them completely. When something is clean of all microbes, it's sterile. But microbes always get back in eventually. We are protected from most of the bad ones by our body's immune system.

# Eye Don't Believe It!

Usually both eyes receive much
the same view of things. You blend these
views into a single three-dimensional picture.
What happens when your eyes receive
different images?

**You will need:**
chairs, hand-held mirror approximately
10 to 15 cm (4 to 6 in) on a side, white
wall or white surface (white poster
board works well), a friend

Rat's Rating

# What to do in this biology experiment

**1** Sit on a chair. Have a white wall on your right. face sideways, towards the white surface.

**2** Have a friend sit very still on a chair a few metres away. They need to be against a plain, light-coloured background.

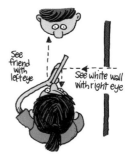

See friend with left eye

See white wall with right eye

**3** Hold the bottom of the mirror with your left hand. Put the mirror edge against your nose. You want the reflecting surface of the mirror to

**4** Keep the mirror edge against your nose and stay very still. Rotate the mirror so that your right eye sees just the reflection of the white wall. And your left eye looks forwards at the face of your friend. Focus on just one feature of their face.

5  Move your hand very
   slowly in front of the
   white surface as if wiping
   a window clean. What
   do you see?

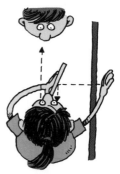

## What Happens

Parts of your friend's face disappear! If this doesn't
work, one of your eyes might be stronger than the
other. Try the experiment again, but this time switch
the eye you use to look at the person and the eye
you use to look at the wall. People vary greatly in
their ability to see this effect. You may have to try
this several times. Give yourself time to see the effect
and don't give up too soon!

It might look as though my eyes have completely disappeared.

But I can still see you!

176

## Why

- Your two eyes usually see very slightly different pictures of the world around you.
- Your brain analyses these two pictures. It then combines them to make a single, three-dimensional image.
- The mirror lets your eyes see two very different views.
- One eye looks straight ahead at your friend. The other eye looks at the white wall and your moving hand.
- Your brain tries to put together a picture that makes sense by selecting bits and pieces from both views.
- Your brain is very sensitive to changes and movement. Since your friend is sitting so still, your brain highlights the information coming from the moving hand, and parts of the face disappear.
- No one knows how or why parts of the face sometimes stay, but the eyes and the mouth seem to be the last features to disappear.

## Fun Fact

You can make an imaginary hole in your hand with just a piece of paper. Roll the paper into a tube with a hole about as big as your eye. Hold it in your right hand and put it up to your right eye. Leave both eyes open, this is very important. Look through the tube. Now put your left hand, fingers up, palm toward your face, up against the left side of the tube, about two-thirds of the way down. Notice that you see a hole in your hand. Your right eye sees the tube and your left eye sees your hand. When these two pictures overlap, the message sent to your brain is that there is a hole in your hand.

## Mini Quiz

In which famous book did a Cheshire cat disappear leaving only its smile behind?

## Mini Answer

The book is *Alice's Adventures in Wonderland* by Lewis Carroll.

# Jelly Belly

Do you only drink a particular type of juice
because you think it tastes best?
Find out if what you see influences what you taste.

**You will need:**
a friend, pairs of jellybeans such
as two cherry, two lime, two lemon,
two orange, plain paper napkins,
cups, pen

Rat's Rating

# What to do in this biology experiment

1  Divide the jellybeans into two groups. Each group should have one of each flavour.

group B have different numbers than the flavours from group A.

2  Label small napkins with the numbers 1–4.

3  Place the jellybeans from group A on a napkin – one jellybean on each napkin.

4  Put the jellybeans from group B into four cups so that your friend can't see them.

5  Label these cups with the numbers 1–4. Make sure that the flavours of

6  Tell your friend the names of the flavours they'll be testing.

7  Get your friend to look at the jellybean on napkin number 1 from group A and then taste the jellybean and write down its flavour. Do the same thing with jellybeans numbered 2 – 4 on the napkins.

8 Keep the colour of the jellybeans in group B hidden. Get your friend to close their eyes and taste the jellybeans. Write down the flavours that your friend says each jellybean tastes like. You can even say that the flavours are the same as before. How many did your friend get right?

## What Happens

When you don't see the colour of the jelly-bean, you often give the wrong answer.

That last one was definitely LEMON!

SORRY! ORANGE!

## Why

- The senses of sight and taste are technically not related. But they can have a strong mental influence on each other.
- Your friend couldn't see the colours of the jelly-beans. Jellybeans don't have a strong smell either. Taste was the only sense left.
- Your taste bud cells have a pit of a very definite shape. When a substance with the matching chemical shape comes along, the receptor cell sends a signal to the brain. This gives the brain clues as to what you are eating.

## Fun Fact

Half fill two drinking glasses with two different flavoured and different coloured soft drinks cherry etc. Half fill another glass with an unflavoured clear (fizzy drink, like sparkling mineral water). Add food colouring to the mineral water. You need a colour to match the colour of one of the flavoured soft drinks. This will make it look like a flavoured soft drink but, of course, it won't have any taste. Get a friend to tell you what each drink tastes like. Chances are they said their unflavoured drink was a flavour that matched the colour.

It doesn't taste like anything... I just drink it for the COLOUR!

## Mini Quiz

Is eyesight important when we eat?

## Mini Answer

In sighted people, eyes are the first sense that decides whether something looks good enough to eat. Colours are very important. Would you eat a blue burger? Food companies add colour to food to make it look better, although the taste stays the same. People like to see foods in colours that they expect. Butter is a pale yellow. But people think butter should be bright yellow, so some manufacturers add yellow colour to the butter.

181

# You've Got a Nerve

How sensitive are you? Try this and see.

## You will need:
coloured pencils, bobby pins, piece of card, compass, scissors, ruler, a friend

Rat's Rating

## What to do in this anatomy experiment

1  With the ruler, mark off 3, 6 and 9 cm (or 1, 2 and 3 in) markings on the card.

2  Use the compass to draw a circle at each of the three markings. You now have three zones – inner, outer and centre.

3  Cut around the outside of the large circle.

4  Colour the zones in three separate colours.

5  Ask your friend to shut their eyes.

6  Stick some bobby pins in the centre zone. Keep the bobby pins at the same height.

7  Press the bobby pins firmly against the arm of your friend. Ask your friend how many bobby pins are felt.

8 Repeat with the bobby pins stuck in the inner and outer zones.

9 Test the skin on the palm, fingers and thumb tips. Which part of your friend's skin is the most sensitive?

## What Happens

The arm is not very sensitive. You can only tell how many bobby pins are in the outer zone. Your palm is less sensitive. You can feel each bobby pin in the inner zone, but not in the centre zone. Your finger-tips are very sensitive. You can feel each one of the bobby pins in the centre zone.

## Why

- Your body is full of nerve endings. These are in your skin and different tissues.
- Parts of your body, including the arm, don't have many nerve endings. It makes it hard for these parts to feel the separate pressures from the bobby pins.
- Your fingers and thumb tips have an extra number of nerve endings. This makes it much easier for you to get accurate results. This is why you feel more pain in areas with more nerve endings.

Most people are ticklish on the bottom of their feet. This is because your feet have such large nerve endings and these make them very sensitive. That is also why a tiny stone in your shoe feels like a rock!

Now I know a rock in my shoe when I feel one... And I feel one now!

## Mini Quiz

Pain relief medicine can stop pain. But how does the medicine know the location of the pain?

## Mini Answer

When you take medicine to stop pain, it doesn't go straight to the pain. It only seems that way, because the pain goes away from the exact spot that hurts! Actually, the pain reliever works with your cells, your nerve endings, your nervous system and your brain to stop you feeling the pain. Some nerve endings can sense pain. When cells in your body are hurt, they let out a chemical. The special nerve endings that sense pain are very sensitive to this chemical. When it is let out, the nerve endings respond. They pick up and send the pain and injury messages through the nervous system to the brain. They tell the brain about the pain, like where it is and how much it hurts. The brain then responds – ouch!

185

# Ghost Fish

You see colours when receptor cells on the retina of your eye are stimulated by light. What happens if your eyes become tired?

**You will need:**
white pieces of card or paper, coloured paper (bright red, green and blue), black marker, scissors, glue

Rat's Rating

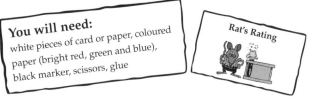

## What to do in this anatomy experiment

1. Draw the same simple fish shape on each of the three coloured papers. Cut out the shape.

2. Glue each shape onto its own white card. Leave one white card blank.

BLANK CARD

3. Draw a small black eye with the marker for each fish. On the last white card, draw the outline of a bowl for your fish.

4. Put the cards in a very bright area (it won't work if you don't!). Stare at the eye of the red fish for 15 to 20 seconds. Then quickly stare at the outline of the bowl. What do you see?

5 Now stare at the eye of the green fish for 15 to 20 seconds. Then quickly stare at the outline of the bowl. What do you see?

6 Finally, do the same with the blue fish. What do you see?

## What Happens

Ghostly fish appear! The red fish is now in the bowl. But its colour has changed to blue-green. The green fish is now in the bowl. But its colour is now red-blue. The blue fish is now in the bowl. And its colour has changed to yellow.

## Why

- The ghostly fish that you see are *afterimages*.
- An afterimage is an image that stays with you even after you have stopped looking at the object.
- The back of your eye is lined with light-sensitive cells called *rods* and *cones*.
- Cones are sensitive to coloured light. Each of the three types of cones is sensitive to a range of colours.
- When you stare at the red fish, the image falls on one area of your retina.
- The red-sensitive cells in that area grow tired. They stop responding strongly to red light.
- The white card reflects red, blue and green light to your eyes. This is because white light is made up of all these colours.
- When you suddenly shift your gaze to the blank white card, the tired red-sensitive cells do not respond to the reflected red light. But the blue-sensitive and green-sensitive cones respond strongly to the reflected blue and green light.
- So, where the red-sensitive cells do not respond you see a bluish-green fish.
- When you stare at the green fish, your green-sensitive cones become tired.
- When you look at the white card, your eyes respond only to the reflected red and blue light, and you see a red-blue fish.
- When you stare at your blue fish, the blue-sensitive cones become tired and your eyes only respond to the reflected red and green light, so you see a yellow fish.

189

# Candle in the Wind

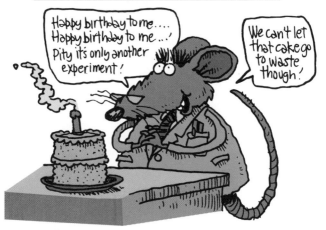

What is the connection between a candle
experiment and the shape of a bird and
aeroplane wing? Find out.

**You will need:**
a candle, low candle holder, cylinder-
shaped container the same height
as the candle (a metal or ceramic
salt shaker is perfect), ADULT
SUPERVISION

Rat's Rating

# What to do in this forces experiment

1. Ask an adult to light a candle. Put it in a low holder and place it on the table.

2. Stand a salt container 8 cm (3 in) in front of the candle.

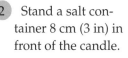

3. Stand on the opposite side of the lit candle. Blow against the container. Make sure you keep your mouth even with the flame of the candle. Do you think you can blow out the candle? Of course not! The container's in the way. Or is it?

## Why
- Air follows the curved shape of the container.
- When the streams of air meet on the other side, they join to blow out the candle.

## Mini Quiz

Why are aeroplane
wings and birds'
wings curved?

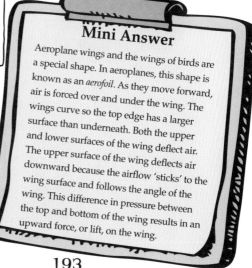

## Mini Answer

Aeroplane wings and the wings of birds are
a special shape. In aeroplanes, this shape is
known as an *aerofoil*. As they move forward,
air is forced over and under the wing. The
wings curve so the top edge has a larger
surface than underneath. Both the upper
and lower surfaces of the wing deflect air.
The upper surface of the wing deflects air
downward because the airflow 'sticks' to the
wing surface and follows the angle of the
wing. This difference in pressure between
the top and bottom of the wing results in an
upward force, or lift, on the wing.

193

# Friendly Apples

An apple a day keeps the doctor away.
But does an apple keep away another apple?

**You will need:**
apples, string

Rat's Rating

## What to do in this air experiment

1. Cut two pieces of string about 1 m (3 ft) each.

2. Tie a piece of string to the stem of each apple.

3. Hang the apples by the string from a clothesline or curtain rod.

4. Hold the apples 5 cm (2 in) apart. What do you think will happen if you blow between the apples? Will they move further apart, pushed by the stream of air? Of course, you think!

5 Blow very hard between the apples.

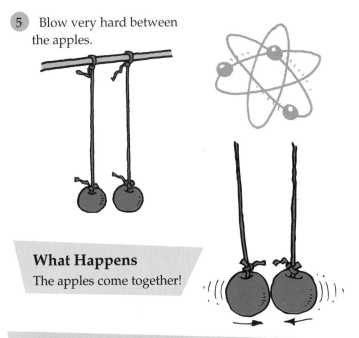

**What Happens**
The apples come together!

## Why
- As the speed of the air gets faster, the pressure of the air gets less.
- When you blow, the air between the apples moves. This means that the air pressure there is less than on the other sides of the apples where the air is still.
- The air on the side of the apples pushes them towards the area of lower pressure and the apples come together.

Lay a bottle with a small mouth on a table. Roll a wad of paper into a pea-sized ball. Put the paper into the mouth of the bottle. Blow hard and fast. Instead of flying into the bottle, the paper flies out at you! Fast moving air goes past the paper and hits the bottom of the bottle. This increases the air pressure inside the bottle. As the compressed air rushes out, it carries the paper with it.

## Mini Quiz

How can a straw work like a bug spray?

## Mini Answer

Half fill a glass of water. Stand a plastic straw upright in the glass. The water will reach as high in the straw as it does in the glass. Hold another straw close to the top of the first straw. Put it at a right angle to the top end of the first straw and blow through it. Watch the water level rise. The fast flowing stream of air makes a decrease in air pressure. Blow very hard. The water rises to the opening and sprays out. You've now atomised the water into fine droplets. Cleaning sprays, insect sprays and perfume atomisers work in the same way.

197

# Smog Alert

Smog is a mix of natural fog – tiny droplets of water in the air and carbon dioxide smoke from pollution. It forms a thick, dirty, smelly atmosphere. Let's make some!

**You will need:**
glass jar, water, aluminium foil, ice cubes, paper, ruler, scissors, matches, ADULT SUPERVISION

Rat's Rating

# What to do in this air experiment

1. Cut a strip of paper about 25 cm x 1.25 cm (10 in x 1/2 in).

2. Fold the length of the strip in half and twist the paper.

3. Make a 'lid' for the glass jar by shaping a piece of aluminium foil over the open end of the jar. Take away the foil and put it aside.

4. Put some water in the jar. Swirl it around so the inside walls of the jar are wet.

5. Pour out the water.

6. Place three ice cubes on top of the foil lid to make it cold.

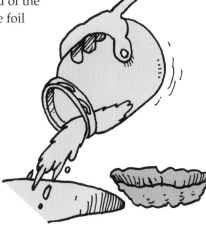

7 Ask an adult to light the strip of paper. Drop it and the match into the damp jar.

8 Quickly put the foil lid on the jar and seal it tightly. Keep the ice cubes on top of the foil, in the middle. What do you see in the jar?

**What Happens**
You have made smog!

## Why

- When you put the lighted paper in the jar, you made some of the water moisture inside the jar evaporate into water vapour.
- The ice made a small amount of the water vapour condense. It turned into droplets of water in the jar. This appears as a mist in the jar.
- Warm damp air meets cold air. The cold air makes the moisture in the warm air condense into tiny droplets that are held in the air. If there is no wind, fog forms.

The city of Los Angeles is very smoggy. At oxygen bars, you can buy pure oxygen. Twenty dollars gets you 20 minutes of plain or fruit-scented oxygen.

Hey buddy...! Give us $100 worth of the Lemon-Lime-Tangerine Dream Oxygen Mix... Better make it snappy ...I'm about to pass out!

THE OXYGEN BAR
LOS ANGELES

## Mini Answer

Smog is harmful to humans, animals and plants. The most harmful parts of smog are ground-level ozone and fine airborne particles. The fog that shrouded London for five days in 1952 caused 4,000 deaths. Road, rail and air transportation stopped. A show at the Sadler's Wells Theatre had to stop because the fog inside made it impossible to see.

## Mini Quiz

Can smog hurt you?

# Where are You?

Can your reflection be here one moment,
then gone the next?

**You will need:**
kitchen foil, scissors

Rat's Rating

## What to do in this light experiment

1 Use the scissors to cut a 25 cm (10 in) length of kitchen foil from the roll. The foil must be smooth. Don't just tear it because it will go as wrinkly as a rat's tail!

2 Look at your reflection on the shiny side of the foil. It won't be perfect, but you'll see yourself quite clearly.

3 Scrunch the foil into a loose ball. Don't press it together tightly because you'll have to flatten it out again.

4 Flatten out the ball of foil

5 Look at your reflection. What do you see?

**What Happens**

Your reflection is gone!

AAHHR...I've vanished!!

## Why

- Light rays reflect from a surface in straight lines.
- When a surface is smooth, the rays are reflected back at you.
- When you make the smooth foil surface all scrunchy, the reflected light bounces off it in all directions.
- Because these reflected rays are going off at different angles, your image does not form in the way it did before.

## Fun Fact

A rainbow is broken into bands of light. The reflection and refraction of the sun's rays in drops of rain make the rainbow. Reflection is simply the return of light waves from the surface of the raindrop. Light that looks white is really a mix of red, orange, yellow, green, blue and violet light.

Unfortunately the rain stopped...and the rainbow disappeared before the guy looking for the pot of gold could find the end of the rainbow...

## Mini Quiz

How can a big shiny spoon turn you upside down?

## Mini Answer

Hold a spoon up so you can see yourself in the scoop. Your reflection is upside down! When light is reflected from a curved surface, the rays leave the surface at different angles. Your reflected image is upside down because of the angle of the reflected rays of light.

205

# Mirror Mirror

When you look in a mirror, you see your reflection.
But how do mirrors reflect light?

**You will need:**
comb, flashlight, piece of heavy paper,
black sheet of paper, hand mirror,
masking tape

Rat's Rating

# What to do in this light experiment

1  Cut a hole in a piece of heavy paper about 2.5 cm (1 in) in diameter.

2  Tape a comb across the hole.

3  Lay a black sheet of paper on the table, or use a dark surface.

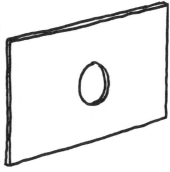

4  Go into a dark room. Place the card with the hole in front of the flashlight so that the narrow beams of light come from the teeth of the comb.

5　Hold a mirror in the beams of light so that it reflects the light.

6　Move the mirror to a different angle. What happens to the beams of light?

**What Happens**

The mirror reflects the light.

## Why

- Light is reflected off the mirror at exactly the same angle as it hits the mirror.
- When you change the angle of the mirror, the angle of the reflected light rays change as well.
- When rays of light hit a surface or an object, they bounce off again. This is called *reflection*.
- Flat shiny surfaces make the best reflections. This is why most mirrors are made of flat sheets of highly polished glass with shiny silver coating behind them.

## Fun Fact

You can write a secret message to friends using mirror code. Put a piece of paper in front of a mirror. Look in the mirror and carefully write your message on the paper. When you look at the paper, you'll see your message back to front in mirror code. Friends will be able to work out the message by looking in their own mirror.

O.K.! You look like a million dollars! PLEASE! I need the mirror now! I've got a very important MIRROR MESSAGE to decode!

## Mini Quiz

If you wave at yourself in a mirror with your left hand, which hand does your reflection use?

## Mini Answer

Your right hand. Mirrors reverse images so that the left side appears to be the right.

# Polar Bear Hair

**What colour is the skin of a polar bear?**

## You will need:
flashlight, clear drinking glass, empty aluminium cans, thermometers, white and black paper, scissors, water, measuring cup, notepaper, pencil

Rat's Rating

## What to do in this light experiment

**1** Shine your flashlight on a clear drinking glass. Does the glass let light pass through? A polar bear's hair lets light through too. The glass also reflects some light. Reflected light makes the polar bear's hair look white.

**2** Some colours are better at soaking up the sun than others. Polar bear skin, under all of that hair, is the colour that absorbs sunlight best. Now, is that colour black or white?

**3** Cover an aluminium can with thick white paper.

**4** Cover another can with black.

**5** Fill each can with 1 cup of water.

**6** Place a thermometer in each cup.

**7** Place both cans in full sun. Tilt them so that as much sunlight as possible hits the sides of the cans. Prop them in place with a book. Then tilt the thermometer so it gets as little direct sunlight as possible.

211

(8) Record the temperature of the water in each can. Record a new temperature every five minutes for 30 minutes. Which colour is best at soaking up the warmth of the sun – white or black? So what colour is the skin of a polar bear?

## What Happens

The water in the black can heats up faster than the water in the white can.

## Why

- Anything dark, like black paper, will soak up more rays of the sun than anything white.
- The light energy is turned into heat.
- The white paper reflects the light before it can turn to heat.
- Polar bear hair and skin are adapted for Arctic climates. Each hair shaft is pigment-free and transparent with a hollow core.
- Polar bears look white because the hollow core scatters and reflects visible light, much like ice and snow.
- When photographed with film sensitive to ultraviolet light, polar bears look black.

## Fun Fact

In 1979, three polar bears at the San Diego Zoo turned green. Scientists found out that algae was growing in the bears' hollow hair shafts. Although the algae didn't harm the bears, killing the algae with a salt solution made their fur white again.

## Mini Quiz

Which gets hotter, land or water?

## Mini Answer

In sunlight, soil heats up faster. Land is darker than water and keeps the heat. In water, the heat goes deeper and spreads. Soil keeps the heat on the surface. If you dig into hot sand on the beach, the sand underneath is cool. Sunlight can't pass through it and the surface stays hot.

# Bright Spark

Who would have thought taking your clothes off in the dark would create an electrical storm!

**Why does the air often crackle when you comb your hair or take off clothes? You'll be 'ecstatic' when you find out.**

## You will need:

a time of year when the air is very dry, winter is a good time (this will not work when the air is humid), scissors, Styrofoam tray from your supermarket (ask at the meat or bakery counter for a clean tray), masking tape, aluminium pie tin

Rat's Rating

## What to do in this electricity experiment

1 Cut a piece from one corner of the Styrofoam tray. You'll have a long bent piece that looks a bit like a hockey stick.

2 Cut a strip of masking tape. Tape the bent piece to the centre of the pie tin to make a handle.

3 Rub the bottom of the Styrofoam tray on your hair. Rub it all over, very fast.

4 Put the tray upside down on a table.

5 Use the handle to pick up the pie tin. Hold it about 30 cm (12 in) over the Styrofoam tray and drop it.

**6** Very slowly, touch the tip of your finger to the pie tin. What happens? Don't touch the Styrofoam tray. If you do, nothing will happen!

## What Happens

You make a bright spark! Use the handle to pick up the pie tin again. Touch the tin with the tip of your finger. You get another great spark. Drop the pie tin onto the Styrofoam tray again. Touch the pie tin. Another spark! Use the handle to pick up the pie tin. More sparks. If the pie tin stops giving you a spark, just rub the Styrofoam tray on your head again, and start over. Try this experiment in the dark. Can you see the tiny lightning bolts you make? What colour are they?

# Why

- When you rub Styrofoam on your hair, you pull electrons off your hair and they pile up on the Styrofoam.
- When you put the aluminium pie tin on the Styrofoam, the electrons on the Styrofoam pull on the electrons from the pie tin.
- Some of the electrons in metals are free electrons. This means they move inside the metal.
- Free electrons try to move as far away from the Styrofoam as they can.
- When you touch the pie tin, the free electrons leap to your hand. They spark!
- The pie tin now has fewer electrons. When you lift the pie tin away from the Styrofoam plate, you have a pie tin that attracts all nearby electrons.

## Fun Fact

In 1752, Benjamin Franklin flew a kite and string in a thunderstorm. The electricity moved down the string. It made a small spark on the metal key near his hand. This showed that lightning was just a big spark of static electricity. He also invented the lightning rod to protect people, buildings and ships from lightning. But, don't try this at home!

Ten seconds after the now-famous lightning bolt hit Benjamin's kite... ... a larger and more powerful bolt closed down his experiment... but drove him to invent the lightning rod.

# Be a Conductor

My faithful old rubber sandal. Are you a CONDUCTOR or an INSULATOR? That is the question!

**Does electricity go through everything? Find out.**

Rat's Rating

## Rat's Helpful Hint
If you're barefooted, don't step on any electric wires. You might get a pair of shocks!

## You will need:
spring type clothes peg, one D-cell battery, aluminium foil or two plastic-covered copper wires, flashlight bulb, masking tape, scissors, ruler, materials to test: safety pin, coins, cork, rubber band, leaf, water, paperclip, glass, plastic

## What to do in this electricity experiment

1. If using copper wires skip to step number 5.

2. Cut the foil into a rectangle 60 cm x 30 cm (24 in x 12 in).

3. Fold the foil in half along its length. Do this five times to make a thin strip 60 cm (24 in) long.

FOLD FOIL TO MAKE ONE STRIP

4. Cut the foil strip in half to make two 60 cm (24 in) strips.

5. Tape one end of both strips to the ends of the battery.

6. Wrap the other end of one strip around the base of the flashlight bulb. Fix the clothes peg around the strip on the end of the light bulb.

7. Test your materials to see if they conduct electricity. Touch the metal tip on the bottom of the flashlight bulb to one side of the material. At the same time, touch the free end of the metal strip to the opposite side of the same material.

TOUCH END OF BULB ON ITEMS TO TEST

## What Happens

Some of your materials will let electricity flow through them and light the bulb. These materials are called *conductors*. Any living thing such as plants, animals and trees are good conductors as well as wire, metal and water. An *insulator* is a material that electricity doesn't easily flow through. Items such as plastic, rubber and glass are good insulators.

## Why

- An electric circuit is the path through which electrons move.
- A switch is a material that acts as a bridge for the electrons.
- When the circuit is closed by a switch, the electrons do not move freely.
- When it is open, the electrons move along the circuit.
- When you touch a good conductor and the tip of the bulb to the other side, you open a circuit.
- The electrons flow from the negative part of the battery through the foil conductor and into the bulb.
- The electrons go from the bulb through the foil and back into the positive end of the battery.
- As long as there is no break in the system, the electrons keep flowing and the bulb stays lit.

## Fun Fact

Electricity is measured in units of power called *watts*. It was named after James Watt, the inventor of the steam engine. One watt is a very small amount of power. It takes nearly 750 watts to equal 1 horsepower. A kilowatt equals 1,000 watts. The waste made by one chicken in its lifetime can supply enough electricity to run a 100-watt bulb for five hours!

## Mini Quiz

Why must you never swim or play outdoors during a thunderstorm?

### Mini Answer

Lightning is a natural form of electricity. You are a good conductor of electricity. Being struck by lightning could kill you.

221

**Want to shock your friends? Here's how!**

You will need:
lemon, paper towels, bowl, coins (copper and non-copper)

Rat's Rating

## What to do in this electricity experiment

1. Squeeze the lemon juice into the bowl.

2. Cut the paper towels into nine 2.5 cm x 5 cm (1 in x 2 in) strips.

3. Soak the strips in the lemon juice.

4. Put down a copper coin. Lay a lemon-soaked strip of paper on top.

5. Put a non-copper coin on top of the paper. Lay a lemon-soaked strip of paper on top.

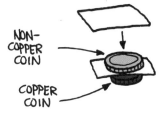

NON-COPPER COIN

COPPER COIN

6 Repeat steps number 4 and 5 until you've made a tower of 10 coins – five copper and five non-copper.

7 Wet one fingertip of each hand.

8 Hold the coin tower between your fingers. What do you feel?

## What Happens

You feel a small shock! This is because you've made a wet cell battery. Wet cells were used before batteries were invented.

## Why

- The different metals in the two types of coins have different electrical strengths in their atoms.
- The lemon juice is a weak acid. It conducts an electric current between the two different coins.
- By having five sets of coins on top of each other, you have increased the electrical voltage of your battery. This is what you do when you put several batteries in a flashlight or radio.
- A battery is two or more dry cells. In each dry cell, 32 metals are separated by blotting paper soaked in a strong acid.